Feeding Jesus

CHRISTIAN POETRY by KAPoe

Feeding Jesus

First published 2012
by KAPoe
Feeding Jesus
©2012 KAPoe

Book Cover Design: AbsoluteCovers.com
Book Layout Designer: Ramesh Kumar Pitchai

ISBN-10: 1480272973
ISBN-13: 978-1480272972
Printed at Createspace.com
(United States of America)

Feeding Jesus

"To order more copies of this book,

please send an email request to

FeedingJesusBook@yahoo.com

with the desired shipping address and you

will receive an email invoice."

✠

Feeding Jesus

KAPoe

Feeding Jesus

Endorsements

I believe that words are expensive. It is language, whether done orally or in written form, that changes the world. Words can inspire, or words can destroy. KAPoe understands the importance of language! I have been touched and inspired by the gift God has given him to speak through poetic language. As you read *Feeding Jesus,* I know you will be touched and inspired too!

KENT PEDERSEN: Senior Pastor, Olive Knolls Church

KAPoe is a man on a mission for the Lord. He is living proof that, "If any man be in Christ, he is a new creation." Having experienced God's grace in his own life, he now blesses others through creative, heartfelt poetry.

JOHN DRAGOUN: Field Director, Prison Fellowship

God has anointed KAPoe with the ability to relate to those who listen to his poems. He reads his poetry each week at Celebrate Recovery in our church, where his word pictures lead us from the tragedies, pain, and hopelessness of

Feeding Jesus

life without God to pointed truths that spring hope and new life into each of us. Each week he receives requests for copies of his poems from those who are touched deeply by the Biblical insights and practical life applications that KAPoe weaves into each piece. I highly recommend this book if you are interested in seeing how God can transform brokenness to life abundant through poetry.

THERON FRIBERG: Associate Pastor, Celebrate Recovery Director

Feeding Jesus

Contents

Feeding Jesus

✚ Contents

Feeding Jesus

Brotherly Love

Feeding Jesus

TRUE BEAUTY

God sees us not as we appear,
As do the eyes of men.
For He looks past the flesh and bones
To beauty deep within.
God helps me see now through His eyes.
True beauty is exposed.
And I can see it bright and clear
Although my eyes are closed.
I see it in a kindly act,
The love of special friends.
I see it in forgiving hearts.
Such beauty knows no end.
We all were ugly ducklings once,
But now those days are gone.
So in the Father's eyes and mine,
You'll always be a swan.

RESCUERS

Listen, Christian soldiers.
We're here to fight a war.
We're recruiters and we're trainers,
And we're clearly something more.
One soldier makes a thousand flee.
His faith they cannot fight.
But with two good soldiers, you and me,
Ten thousand take to flight.
Now I'm no mathematician,
But it sure seems to me,
There're plenty faithful troops on Earth
If we could just agree.
Then adorned in spiritual armor,
With our helmets, shields, and swords,
Marching fearlessly into the world
We'll rescue prisoners of war.
We'll bring them back upon our shoulders.
A hero's welcome they'll receive.
And when they see how much God loves them,
How could they not believe?

Brotherly Love ✝ Rescuers

12

RECONCILIATE

"COME UNTO ME. BE RECONCILED,"
Said God from high above.
"I'VE WASHED YOUR EVERY SIN AWAY.
REPLACED, THROUGH GRACE, WITH LOVE.
I BID MY FAMILY WELCOME YOU,
EMBRACE AND HOLD YOU FAST.
AND THAT THEY JUDGE YOU BY YOUR FRUIT,
NOT BY YOUR SINFUL PAST."
For reconciliation means,
to God, you're new this day.
The one you used to be is dead,
Forever cast away.
A friend of God. A long lost son.
So slay the fatted calf.
Adorn the ring, the shoes, and robe.
Rejoice in his behalf!
For God alone will choose the sheep
that enter by the gate.
It's ours to stand, arms open wide,
And reconciliate.

Brotherly Love ✝ Reconciliate

KAPoe

13

FEEDING JESUS

When did we feed Your hunger, Lord?
I can't recall, I think.
When did we find You thirsty,
and give to You to drink?
Lord, when were You a stranger?
When did our homes we share?
When did we find You naked,
and give You clothes to wear?
When did You have infirmity?
When were You in a cell,
That we should come to visit You,
or help to make You well?
The Lord says, "Help My brothers.
For I'm in them, you see?
But if you turn your back on them,
you walk away from Me."
The prison's not a man made hell
but an infirmary.
And disciples are the doctors
that help the blind to see.
The harvest there is plentiful.
The laborers are few.
If Jesus is your Lord of lords,
then He is sending you.

KAPoe

Embracing them when they emerge,
We lead them to reward.
And all the love and care we show,
we show to our Sweet Lord.

Feeding Jesus

STONE THROWERS

The crowd brought an adulteress.
The Law said she must die.
A sin that blood from beasts can't hide
from God's most holy eye.
Christ said, "Let him who never sinned
be first to cast his stone."
And this, before the blood of Christ,
gave power to atone.
The righteousness of God's a gift.
Our own is but a curse,
Deceiving us to think we're good,
and other folks are worse.
The Savior bled to cleanse us all
of sins He must despise.
Though none are worthy, all may come.
We're perfect in His eyes.
Christ died that sinners might be saints.
We're nothing on our own.
Don't stand knee deep in Jesus' blood
and keep on throwing stones.

KAPoe

THE LOVE SEEN

The family of God is ours.
Moms, dads, sisters, and brothers.
We share God's love with all on Earth,
But these far more than others.
The world sees Christ alive in us
through love of family.
For God is love, and He's exposed
for all the world to see.
We ache to bless the family
that we love in the Lord.
Because it fills our hearts with joy,
and this is our reward.
Don't allow your pride to push away
the blessings of their love.
You'll steal their joy and break their hearts
and sadden God above.
God's wisdom uses all of us
to set His blessings free.
And love becomes the glue that bonds
His precious family.
When others see such deep, true love
their hearts have never known,
they'll run to God with open arms
and fall before His throne.

KAPoe

Feeding Jesus

SHARE

God wants to give us all good things.
But, sadly, He cannot.
For we put too much hope and trust
in that which we have got.
We cling so tightly to our lack,
And there we put our faith.
But what we give, God multiplies,
then gives it back through grace.
So share the little that you have
for other lives to touch.
Be faithful with a little,
and God will give you much.
God's searching for those faithful ones,
For them He wants to bless.
Because, like Him, it's on their heart
to share it with the rest.
Why should God bless a selfish man
who clings to all in greed
When He can bless a faithful man
who finds and meets a need?

KAPoe

GENTLE SPIRITS

If in your heart you know God's Word,
that sets you not above.
A scholar is a useless tool,
unless he acts in love.
God says "the unsaved man is blind."
His heart can't see the Light.
And only love can cure him now
that he may gain his sight.
Your goal to win the argument
might prove that you are smart.
But kind and loving, gentle words
are how you'll win his heart.
When we condemn a sinful man,
it's Satan's grand reward.
But if we lead this man in love
the treasure is the Lord's.
A gentle spirit's led by love
and not by vain conceit.
Unforgiving hearts don't point unto the mercy seat.
So open up your heart each day
that you'll gently restore.
The man who is forgiven much
will love God all the more.

Isaiah 42:16

Brotherly Love ✚ Gentle Spirits

Make It Right

You're my brother, and I love you.
My acts are meant in kind.
In hopes that I will not offend,
in love, I speak my mind.
If offended by my brother,
I will place that in the light.
By putting it before his eyes
our love can make it right.
The Lord says love your neighbor
but your brother all the more.
We stand as one through all attacks
that Satan has in store.
Because no man is perfect,
in humbleness we live.
The family of God can't stand
unless our hearts forgive.

Brotherly Love ✚ Make It Right

KAPoe

Feeding Jesus

ABUNDANT SEED

His sign said, "I'm down on my luck,
and I will work for food."
A talk between my Lord and me,
within my mind, ensued.
I said, "Dear God, please guide me now
and show me this man's need."
He said, "CHILD OPEN UP YOUR HEART
AND PLANT ABUNDANT SEED."
I told the man, "I'm here today
to do the Father's will," and then I handed to the man
a hundred dollar bill.
Next day, the man came up to me,
Great tears within his eyes.
He asked me to forgive him now,
Confessing of his lies.
He said he didn't need the cash
but chased an ill reward.
He said my gift melted his heart
and drove him to the Lord.
"I'm here to bring your money back.
So take it now I plead."
I took it, and I thanked the Lord
for meeting my great need.

Brotherly Love ✠ Abundant Seed

KAPoe

21

Feeding Jesus

BLESS THE SAINTS

Without the saints, where would we be?
Their kindness lifts and comforts me.
They help us out along the way.
Sometimes they know just what to say.
I know the Spirit's guiding them
To help us answer life's problems.
They lead our hearts to recognize
Things God wants us to realize.
They know God's Word.
Their hearts are warm.
They lead their brothers through the storm.
They're not the angels though, you see,
But Christian folks like you and me.

KAPoe

COMMON GOALS

How can two souls walk side by side
And share a common bond
With opposition of the heart
That they can't get beyond?
If they are prone to disagree
And can't see eye to eye,
What point is there to choose a friend
On whom they can't rely?
How can they share a common goal
With different points of view?
Please tell me how two so opposed
Can make that dream come true?
If you can't yield unto a friend,
Content to stand at odds.
If your opinion's all that counts,
Then you won't honor God's.
If you're determined in this life
To always be the boss,
Then you can't hope to serve the Lord,
And that will be your loss.
So let the Lord soften your heart.
Don't be so quick to scoff.
When God is Master in your life,
You'll be much better off.

KAPoe

Feeding Jesus

I Love You

"I love you" is so easy said.
They're simple words to say.
But true love can be seen and felt.
It guides your every way.
We all know who the Christians are
By blessings they impart.
You can't ignore a neighbor's needs
When God lives in your heart.
If you abide in Jesus Christ
And He abides in you,
Then His love will be apparent
In everything you do.
To the cold one give a blanket.
And those who hunger, feed.
But don't ever want repayment.
Trust God to meet your need.
When you give love, you give them God.
For love is what He is.
A simple gesture from your heart
Could lead them to be His.

KAPoe

I'M PURPLE

I wish we all were purple.
Then everywhere we'd go
There'd be no way to judge someone
We really didn't know.
Then everyone would get a chance
To show what's in their heart.
There'd be no cause for bigotry
That drives the world apart.
I'm glad the Lord is color blind
Where people are concerned.
Because the color of our skin
Is not something that's earned.
He'll only judge by faith and works
And by the love we show.
Then if our name is in His book,
That's all He needs to know.
God created all men equal.
So on the judgment day,
The new shell that He gives us
Might be purple anyway.

KAPoe

Feeding Jesus

KAPoe

Feeding Jesus

Faith

Feeding Jesus

Faith ✚ Contents

KAPoe

STORMS

Sometimes we must face storms in life.
.The Lord may send us there.
Because He knows experience
Will help us to prepare.
Then when the storm is at its worst,
Where fear and anguish breed,
He'll walk on water if He must
To be there in our need.
If we have faith in only Him
And not upon the waves,
We'll walk upon the water too,
Unto the One Who saves.
But we must concentrate on Him
So that our faith won't shrink.
For if we take our eyes off Him,
Then we will start to sink.
And when we cry to Him in fear
We know He'll understand.
And though we bring it on ourselves,
He lends a helping hand.
He takes us back then to our boat.
From wind and rain we've spurned.
We realize the storm was good
Because of what we've learned.

Faith ✝ Storms

KAPoe

Feeding Jesus

SAFETY NETS

I always had a "just in case"
When I'd step out in faith.
A "just in case" it's not His will,
A safety net in place.
Time after time I'd miss the mark,
and landed in the net.
It happened far too many times.
And so I got upset.
I turned to God and questioned Him.
"Why did You let me fall?
I'm expecting You to catch me when
I'm answering Your call."
"YOU SHOW UP TO THE FEAST I SPREAD
WITH YOUR SACK LUNCH IN HAND.
SO YOU MUST EAT THE FOOD YOU BRING
UNTIL YOU UNDERSTAND.
I LONG TO HOLD YOU IN MY ARMS
AND COMFORT YOU THROUGH GRACE.
BUT CHILD, YOU PUSH MY ARMS AWAY
WHEN YOU DON'T COME IN FAITH."

KAPoe

One Dark Day

Her doctor told her, one dark day,
He had bad news to give.
There was no easy way to say
She hadn't long to live.
She told me and tears filled my eyes
So I could hardly see.
She held me in her loving arms
And tried to comfort me.
I go to see her every day,
And much to my surprise,
She's up and dressed and cleaning house.
Such joy is in her eyes.
The inner strength of ten brave men
Has been hers from the start.
Such victory she claims each day
With Jesus in her heart.
Through faith in God she marches on,
Her countenance aglow.
No matter what her doctor said
Some seven years ago.

KAPoe

Feeding Jesus

My Thorn

I've hidden my infirmity
that no one else may see,
In fear of what the world might say
And what they'll think of me.
I cannot bear their ridicule.
They judge me unconcerned
of pain I live with day by day.
They say my plight I've earned.
And so I turn to God in prayer.
In Him will I confide.
What must I do that You'll remove
the thorn here from my side?
He said, "THERE'S NOTHING YOU CAN DO
BUT THAT YOU JUST BELIEVE
THAT YOU CAN TRUST ME FOR THE GIFT
REPENTANT SOULS RECEIVE."
And so, in faith, I ask again.
For in His grace I stand.
And then I, in humility,
stretch out my withered hand.

KAPoe

SWEET MUSIC

A cry for help is music
unto the Savior's ears
Because it shows we trust Him
with all our greatest fears.
He loves the hallelujah
I give Him when He's done.
But desperate cries reveal I know
He loves me as a son.
He wants to be the hero
that meets our greatest need.
That's why He came to Earth to die,
to suffer and to bleed.
I think the greatest praise we give
is calling on His name
And trusting Him to clear our sin,
our guilt, and all our shame.
He may just bring that trial Himself
and wait for you to call.
So He can spread His mighty arms
and catch you when you fall.

Faith ✚ Sweet Music

KAPoe

Feeding Jesus

UNLIMITED

If you don't have joy in life
you're doing something wrong.
If you live in misery,
your faith is not that strong.
Do you have more faith in the past
than you have in God's Word?
God says "your past is cast away
and that, through grace, you're cured."
You think your past is too extreme?
Too violent, lewd, or odd?
And, since you feel so overwhelmed,
that it's too big for God?
Do you believe God made the Earth,
the sun, and moon, and stars?
He formed you in your mother's womb,
And He can heal your scars.
He says, "In Christ we do all things."
We must believe it's true.
Don't put more limits on the Lord
Than He has put on you.

KAPoe

You Know Best

There is much upon my heart right now
I feel the need to say.
I ask that You forgive me, God,
for foolish things I've prayed.
Don't answer all my questions, Lord,
But make me trust Your grace.
It's only when I do not know
that I rely on faith.
Don't give me what I ask for, God,
in ignorance or greed.
But in Your wisdom do Your will
Because You know my need.
Please help me to be still, my Lord,
and listen for Your voice
That You may put it on my heart
to make the proper choice.
It's when I think I know the way
I make the biggest mess.
It's when, in faith, I follow You
that I am truly blessed.

Feeding Jesus

Make It Rain

A farmer, on his knees, in tears,
prayed, "Please, God, make it rain.
Without Your blessings on the land
I cannot grow the grain.
I read and live Your Word each day.
I've prayed most faithfully.
Please help me, Lord, to save my farm
and feed my family."
The farmer fasted forty days.
He scarcely left his knees.
His shirt was wet from all his tears.
He prayed, "My Savior, please."
Then, through an angel in the night,
the Father sent to speak,
He said, "My heart is aching, son,
to give you what you seek.
I know that you believe I'll send
the rain you hope to yield.
I'm waiting till you show the faith
to go and plow your fields."

KAPoe

WORLDLY EYES

As those who looked with worldly eyes
upon the cross that day,
they could not see the Lord's great plan.
So felt compelled to say,
"This cannot be the holy Christ
that on this cross is nailed.
He died before He saved us all.
We see that He has failed."
They couldn't see that our sweet Lord
did what He came to do.
He healed, restored, and opened eyes
Then died for me and you.
Because their worldly thoughts and goals
were not the same as His,
they only saw defeat that day,
and said, "That's all there is."
Through worldly eyes they couldn't see
the things the heart was shown.
They missed the greatest victory
the world has ever known.

KAPoe

CHARIOTS

Sometimes the trials we face in life
are chariots of gold.
But through our lack of faith we shun
the treasures that they hold.
God fills them with His riches.
Great wisdom He imparts.
But our eyes see them as evil,
And terror fills our hearts.
So we must face our demons
and climb right up inside.
We grab the whirlwind by the reins
and then brace for the ride.
The other choice is just to faint
and fall down in it's path.
In weakness, treasures God has sent,
received in pain as wrath.
So recognize the rocky paths
as trails to reward.
We'll choose to cower, rant or cry,
or glorify the Lord.

KAPoe

EVIL DARTS

The devil draws his mighty bow,
His arrows shot at will.
He shoots them to cause strife and pain.
Sometimes he shoots to kill.
So many targets for his bow,
he scarcely needs to aim.
Each arrow labeled with a plight,
like guilt or fear or shame.
I see his victims falling fast.
They crumble in despair.
Their hearts and souls cry out in pain,
but Satan doesn't care.
Into the light the arrows fly
that He shoots from the dark.
But they land gently at my feet.
They cannot hit their mark.
So as he's shooting more, in vain,
as though he's shooting blind,
He hears a voice from Heaven say,
"I TOLD YOU, THIS ONE'S MINE."

Feeding Jesus

EYES FRONT

How can we run a race for God
while looking at the past?
If you can't see where you're going,
you're going nowhere fast.
God says, "Throw off what hinders."
The weight of things past done.
For we must lighten our great load
before we start to run.
So whether it's the things you've done
or what's been done to you.
The future is a narrow path.
The past just won't fit through.
Keep your eyes on Christ, Who leads,
And move ahead through grace.
But if you're living in the past,
you're just running in place.
There is no future in the past.
Your joy can't be complete.
You'll have to pick between the two.
The twain shall never meet.

KAPoe

Feeding Jesus

Hell Believes

I told a friend, "Come unto God,
His mercy to receive."
He said, "I have no time for that
because I don't believe."
"Please tell me, then, what purpose is
there in this life you live?"
The man just shrugged his shoulders.
No answer could he give.
"How sad to think you know not God,
Who made you with intent.
And that you think you're here for nought.
You're just an accident.
Our purpose is to serve the Lord.
To you that seems a chore.
But once your heart knows His great love,
you'll want to serve Him more.
Way deep down in the depths of Hell
no unbelievers be.
Each soul that's there believes in God.
But now, too late, they see."

KAPoe

Feeding Jesus

JUMP

I'm standing high upon the roof.
The building burns below.
The flames rise up to lick my face
whichever way I go.
I hear my Father calling me.
He waits with open arms.
He beckons me to jump to Him.
He seeks to spare me harm.
I pause in fear. I gasp for air.
My eyes burn from the smoke.
My faith grows weak. I don't comply
to words my Father spoke.
I say, "I cannot see You there.
The smoke has made me blind."
My Father says, "I'M HERE BELOW,
AND I CAN SEE JUST FINE."
Through courage I receive from Him
I leap out into space.
I look up from His loving arms
to see His smiling face.

Faith ✚ Jump

KAPoe

MANY QUESTIONS

Who am I that God would see me?
Why does the Father care?
Why does He love me so completely?
Why does, my life, He want to share?
How can He know my deepest secrets?
Why did His only Son He send?
How did He know my heart so needed
simple love from special friends?
Why does He prove Himself to me?
Why does He bless me so?
Why would He want to guide my steps
all places I might go?
Why does He build a house for me?
Or save me from the fire?
Why did He dirty holy hands
to reach into my mire?
There's just one answer for these things.
In all that I receive,
God shows me His undying love
because my heart believes.

KAPoe

Feeding Jesus

Above It All

I stood upon a lofty cliff
That faced a restless sea.
Above the water was my God,
There beckoning to me.
I pondered how to get to Him.
I searched for ways to go.
The waves crashed on the jagged rocks
A hundred feet below.
He said, "JUST KEEP YOUR EYES ON ME,
AND DO JUST WHAT I SAY.
HAVE FAITH, I'LL NEVER TELL YOU, COME,
AND THEN NOT MAKE A WAY."
I thought, if I can't trust the Lord,
I may as well be dead.
And so I ventured from the cliff
Just as my Father said.
His hand comes up to meet my feet
When I step out in faith,
Enabling me to do His will
By virtue of His grace.

KAPoe

Always Hope

Our God knew all His children
Before the Earth was here.
He knew who would reject Him
And who would love Him dear.
He knows that we are stubborn.
He knows how hard we'll fight.
And how much torment we must face
Before we'll see the Light.
He doesn't want to punish you.
But He'll do what He must
To show you there's no other Way.
And Him you need to trust.
You've made your choices in this life.
Great patience God has shown.
He didn't cause your misery.
You've done this on your own.
When you feel like you can't go on,
You need not go that far.
For God will fill your heart with joy
No matter where you are.
If it seems that there's no hope
And nothing more to lose,
There's still a chance for victory.
Be careful what you choose.
You've tried to find true happiness

Faith ✝ Always Hope

Feeding Jesus

In substance or romance.
Admit those vain attempts have failed,
And give the Lord a chance.
So take this painful life you live
And give it to the Lord.
Then through His wisdom, grace and love,
All hope can be restored.

Faith ✚ Always Hope

KAPoe

ANSWER HIS CALL

Don't be afraid to step out on the water.
Don't be afraid to reach out for His hand.
For when you know the Spirit calls you to it,
The water is the safest place to stand.
Sometimes you must ignore your worldly knowledge
And push man's understanding from your head.
Our Lord can keep you safer in the war zone
Than you thought you were when you were home in bed.
Our Savior, Who's within you, is your power
To do the things that you don't think you can.
You'll come to know that you can count as foolish
The rules of science that discourage man.
For nothing is impossible through Jesus.
He's proven these words time and time again.
Faith in God can bring us to the victory
Over what is deemed impossible by man.
When you know that you've received your calling,
It's there and then that you must make your stand.
You'd best believe that He will see you through it.
For the outcome's preordained within His plan.

KAPoe

BELIEVE

If you have faith things will go wrong
And speak it from the heart,
Then prepare yourself for failures.
Your world will fall apart.
If you say this headache's killing me,
Then perhaps this headache will.
Don't speak destruction out in faith
For our God to fulfill.
If you have faith that's positive,
You'll move the mountain true.
But if you trust the negative,
Then mountains fall on you.
And if you say that you have faith
But don't feel it inside,
Then you'll be stuck depending on
Those other ways you've tried.
You must believe our gracious God
Does not want you to fail.
You've got to trust Him from the heart,
And then you can prevail.

KAPoe

BLIND FAITH

Our faith is only blind at first,
The way it needs to be.
But as we study God's sweet Word,
Our hearts begin to see.
The more we read, the more we see
The sacrifice He's made.
And as we meditate there on,
The darkness starts to fade.
His Word provides a brilliant Light
To guide the steps we take.
It gives us wisdom that we need
For choices we must make.
He knows we'll stumble as we go.
He lifts us lovingly.
He leads us back unto the place
He knows we need to be.
In time His Light so fills our hearts,
And glows so splendidly,
That we must place It on a stand
For all the world to see.

Faith ✟ Blind Faith

KAPoe   49

COULD WE? WOULD WE?

Christians give their lives to God.
We hear this constantly.
So I've prepared some questions.
They're meant to help us see.
What if God let your children die?
Not two or three, but ten.
How would that affect your walk?
Could you still love Him then?
What if God took all your cattle
That provides your livelihood?
And when your sorrow dragged you Home,
Your house no longer stood.
Would you fall right down and worship God,
And give Him all your praise?
And would it still fulfill your heart
To give Him all your days?
I hope our answers would be yes.
We're still prepared to give our best.
But don't let your answer make you smug.
You haven't heard the rest.
Now your skin dries up in painful sores
From your feet up to your crown.
And you have to scrape them constantly
To keep infection down.
Then your spouse and friends admonish you

KAPoe

Feeding Jesus

For your faith in God above.
Would you scold them harshly
And still give God your love?
Bountiful Heaven's treasures,
From such faith, we'd expect.
But if you didn't know that
Could you still maintain respect?

Faith ✠ Could we? Would we?

Feeding Jesus

God Help Me

He got up two hours earlier
and kissed his loving wife.
A very important meeting that day
was going to change their life.
As he said his morning prayer
he asked the Lord to grant him speed.
"My timing must be right today.
Please meet my special need."
But then as he was getting dressed,
he looked down, one sock was blue.
And when he found a pair that matched,
he couldn't find his shoe.
Then when he was prepared to leave
he couldn't find his keys.
With anger in his voice he said,
"God, won't You help me please!?"
As he was racing to the airport,
a brand new tire went flat.
He slammed the door and yelled at God,
"You could have spared me that!"
Then arriving at the airport
about ten minutes late,
They said that he had missed his flight
and that he'd have to wait.
..then, finally, he arrived, at last.

KAPoe

Feeding Jesus

His appointment time, one hour past.
A note handed him at the meeting room
said, "Sorry we're late, we'll be there soon."
As he fell relieved into a chair,
his cell phone's ringing filled the air.
His wife said a news flash on TV
said his first flight crashed into the sea.

Faith ✚ God Help Me

Feeding Jesus

KAPoe

Feeding Jesus

Forgiveness

Forgiveness ✚ Contents

Feeding Jesus

KAPoe

Feeding Jesus

Muddy Boots

An inmate knelt down by his bunk
To end a rainy day.
The same way he did every night,
He closed his eyes to pray.
Another man, wet from the storm,
Whose view of Christ was dim,
Removed his muddy, rain-soaked boots,
Then threw them both at him.
He said, "You Christians make me sick!
You're stuck in here like me.
If Jesus is so wonderful,
Why won't He set you free!?"
The Christian man, not looking up,
Continued praying deep.
The angry man lay on his bunk
And soon fell fast asleep.
When dawn had broken he awoke.
And much to his surprise,
His boots sat polished at his feet.
His warm tears filled his eyes.
His soul convicted of his sin.
His heart was changed that day.
Then kneeling down upon the floor
The man began to pray.

KAPoe

Forgiveness ✟ Muddy Boots

Feeding Jesus

The Other Wayward Son

Are you the older brother
who will not recognize
The Father's grace for someone else
whose sins that you despise?
Does it make you feel noble
when you just can't forgive
some certain sin of someone else
or how they used to live?
Then you're conforming to the world.
You've tossed God's Word aside.
Has this sin become some honor badge
that you display with pride?
If you want the Lord's forgiveness
and blessings as you go,
then that must be the crop you plant.
We reap just what we sow.
You can't be more moral than God.
Don't place yourself above.
For that was Satan cast to Earth
by the Father of all love.

KAPoe

WALLS

We must build the Father's house
with love and not with pride.
For if we build the walls too high,
the world can't see inside.
The Great Physician says to "COME,
BE CLEANSED OF ALL YOUR SIN."
The only god we serve is self
if we don't let them in.
The church is not a country club,
where perfect Christians dwell.
It's not our place to pick and choose
who Christ should save from Hell.
If we're to be the arms of God,
we must be open wide.
And we must lift the sinners high
and carry them inside.
It's good that God's house has a roof
to protect us from the squalls.
But we can't truly serve the Lord
till we tear down the walls.

Feeding Jesus

WELCOME

We welcome all who come to God
to worship at His throne.
Because we know no sin they bear
is greater than our own.
God washes all our sins away.
He doesn't pick and choose.
Our Savior died for all of us.
He bled to pay our dues.
So come each vile, perverted wretch,
whose sins are brash and real.
For you're the very souls the Great
Physician came to heal.
So bring repentant souls, confessed,
that God picks from the crowd.
But to this rule we must adhere…
No perfect folks allowed.

60   KAPoe

FORGIVE

If God forgives them, why can't you?
Are you greater than He?
Or would you teach the Lord Himself
about morality?
If God says yes, but you say no,
you call the Lord a liar.
And you seek not to please our God
But just your own desire.
Don't doubt God's power to change a man
through grace earned by His Son.
Don't doubt that God can bring them home,
no matter what they've done.
Our God created everything
on Earth and all above.
There is no heart that He can't change
through virtue, faith, and love.
So if you still have doubts about
what you think God can do.
I'll worry not, for I have faith
that He can change you too.

Forgiveness ✝ Forgive

FORGIVE YOURSELF

When God says, "I'VE FORGIVEN YOU,"
How dare you not comply?
If you won't trust His wisdom there,
On whom will you rely?
He knows your guilt's an anchor
That's heavy on your chest.
He knows that you're unworthy.
Through grace the sinner's blessed.
He chooses to forget your sins,
Forever cast away.
Don't force Him to remember them
By what you think or say.
If you will not forgive yourself,
Then you reject His love.
When your opinion matters most
You place yourself above.
It's only through the Father's love
That people overcome.
If you're waiting till you're worthy,
That day will never come.
Unforgiveness is a sin,
Although the sinner's you.
Don't listen to the devil's lies.
Each day God's mercy's new.

KAPoe

Feeding Jesus

It's God's acceptance that you seek,
And everybody else.
But victory eludes your heart
Till you forgive yourself.

Feeding Jesus

Feeding Jesus

God's Love

God's Love ✚ Contents

Feeding Jesus

KAPoe

TRUE LOVE

Love is the perfect gift God gave,
The Son that He'd begot.
Love is the sacrifice He made
for those who knew Him not.
Love is the jealousy God feels
for those who never pray.
Love is the tears He'll cry for them
when comes the judgment day.
Love is His pity felt for those
who laughed His Son to scorn.
Love is the lashes He endured,
by which His flesh was torn.
Love cries and aches and suffers long
for those who know the Lord.
Love sweats and bleeds in sacrifice,
expecting no reward.
Love is the main ingredient
that makes this life superb.
But love's not just a tender thought.
My friends, love is a verb.

God's Love ✝ True Love

KAPoe

THE WORDS OF A THIEF

It's no secret this Man's innocent
Who hangs upon the tree.
And though I've earned my fate this day,
He suffers more than me.
What kind of Man would pray for them
Who torture Him this way?
He asks that God would charge them not
For crimes they've done this day.
No holy man in all this land
Has faith that this Man shows.
I've asked Him to remember me
When He gets where He goes.
He says that I will be with Him
No matter what I've done.
There is no doubt within my heart
That He's the Father's Son.

KAPoe

IMAGINE GOD

When someone struggles by the way,
I long to lend a hand.
Imagine God, Who wants to help,
But has a greater plan.
I long for friends from far away.
One day, I wish they'd share.
Imagine God, the Deity,
Who longs for just a prayer.
I see one with a broken heart.
A tear flows from my eye.
Imagine how the Father feels,
Who loves far more than I.
When trials strike our family
And anguished hearts befall,
Imagine God with arms stretched wide
Enough to hold us all.

God's Love ✚ Imagine God

KAPoe

Feeding Jesus

Feeding Jesus

Grace

Feeding Jesus

KAPoe

GRACE RIVER

There is a river deep and wide
that flows through all the Earth.
It is the special gift from God
to those of His rebirth.
Anyone can swim in there
if they believe it's good.
It's waters bless and heal and love
if they believe it could.
The world builds bridges over it.
They cross it high above.
They fear they'll drown within its depths,
So they deny God's love.
The waters give us joy and life.
They cleanse us of all sin.
We are the righteousness of God
the moment we step in.
I'm swimming backstrokes in His love.
A smile adorns my face.
My Lord declares me innocent
in God's river of grace.

KAPoe

Feeding Jesus

UNFORSAKEN

I'm moved, in spirit, to the cross.
For, there, my God has taken me.
My perfect Savior asks of God,
"Why have You forsaken Me?"
For He had lived a perfect life,
Of shame there was no trace.
And He deserved the grand reward
we only get through grace.
But we deserve no grand reward
But rather shame and loss.
Though Jesus had earned Heaven's best,
the rest have earned the cross.
But God gives not what we deserve.
His mercy grants good things.
He lets us in His family,
And all of Heaven sings.
So now I stand, arms open wide.
In righteousness, God dressed me.
And there I cry out to the Lord,
"God, why have You so blessed me?"

KAPoe

Feeding Jesus

UNCONDITIONAL

I think most folks don't understand
love unconditional.
Or how much love it really takes
for hearts to be that full.
God sent His only Son to die
for all His enemies.
To shed the only blood there is
that truly sets them free.
Each time the lash lay 'cross His back,
Each time His flesh was torn,
His heart cried out, "I love you, child.
I pray you'll be reborn."
They cursed His name and spit on Him.
Such hell they put Him through.
And so He prayed, "Forgive them God.
They know not what they do."
God, let my heart hold love so true.
May my heart be so full.
That self and pride cannot dissuade
love unconditional.

KAPoe

75

Grace ✚ Unconditional

Feeding Jesus

GOD'S WRATH

Elijah called upon the Lord
to show His righteous might.
He sent His fire from above
within the people's sight.
Under the Law, God's wrath consumed
the water and the ox.
Upon the alter naught remained.
He even burned the rocks.
But then God sent His Son to Earth,
To us, His holy gift.
He came to bleed and then to die
The curse that He might lift.
We mocked Him, and we tortured Him,
Our Sacrifice to be.
And so the Lord laid down His life
that He might set us free.
We hung Him on the cross that day
to bare the sins of man.
But under grace the wrath of God
did not consume the Lamb.

KAPoe

THE GOD OF
SECOND CHANCES

God loves His children more than we
will ever understand.
He knows we can't walk perfect lines
laid out through His commands.
That's why God's plan includes His grace,
The hope we have to live.
And when our hearts return to Him,
He's eager to forgive.
And that forgiveness He instills
within our hearts as well,
That we will long to lift the one
who somehow tripped and fell.
Like the Father on the rooftop
awaits His son's return,
we must extend the arms of God,
through grace that none can earn.
God's grace and love are never based
on sin nor circumstance.
Based only on what's in our hearts,
God grants another chance.

KAPoe

DENOUNCING GRACE

God, please forgive my brothers
for looking down on me.
Condemning me for things I did
before You set me free.
Forgive them, Lord, for doubting
that You could make me new.
Please show them that by judging me
they're also judging You.
Please quench the great accuser,
who leads their hearts this day.
But if they can't forgive me,
please forgive them anyway.
I pray, please hedge them from the world
before conforming starts.
And may they be transformed
by the renewing of their hearts.
Please show them they're not fit to judge.
They cannot take Your place.
For when they judge what You forgave
then they're denouncing grace.

KAPoe

CHANGED

Not only have You changed my heart
But, God, you've changed my mind.
I see so clear how wrong I was.
You've shown me I was blind.
So backwards was what I believed.
My life was such a mess.
So much seems right unto a man
That in the end brings death.
I thought Christians were misguided
And easily deceived.
T'was I who fell for Satan's lies
And as a fool believed.
I don't deserve the happiness
You give me day by day.
What I deserve is death and hell,
My sinful debt to pay.
You sacrificed for my great sin
The Son whom you'd begat.
And though I'm guilty for His death,
You forgave me even that.

Grace ✚ Changed

KAPoe

Feeding Jesus

A USEFUL VESSEL

I used to be a better pot
of beauty, strength, and pride,
A useful vessel men could trust
with all they placed inside.
But now a pot with many cracks,
Unpleasant to the eye,
Unuseful in my brokenness
no matter how I try.
But God sees me as beautiful
through eyes of love and grace.
Great treasures then He placed in me:
His Spirit, hope, and faith.
I begged, "Lord, mend the cracks and holes
that soil my good name.
Please make me as I was before
that I might hide my shame."
"I CHOSE YOU WITH THOSE CRACKS AND HOLES
CAUSED BY YOUR LIFE OF SIN.
AND IT'S THROUGH THEM THE WORLD MIGHT SEE
THE LIGHT I'VE PLACED WITHIN."

KAPoe

At The Well

I walk along the silent road.
Unto the well alone.
For no one wants my company
Even among my own.
I've led a life of sin and shame
I know I can't live down.
I cannot bear the angry stares.
My face turns to the ground.
A weary Man sits at the well,
A holy Man, I think.
He speaks to me in gentle words
and asks me for a drink.
He tells me of my evil past
and every sin I've sought.
Yet in His voice I sense great love.
His words condemn me not.
A gift from God, He offers me,
that new life might begin.
A living water I can drink
and never thirst again.
I run to town and tell the crowd,
"Make haste to see the One.
The great Messiah we await.
The Father's only Son."

KAPoe

Feeding Jesus

MIRACLES OF GRACE

Lord, help me to stay awe-struck
by blessings I receive.
And keep me in amazement
of the God whom I believe.
Don't let me be complacent
with all the gifts You give
That lead my heart to praise You
through all the days I live.
Please lead my heart to recognize
Your miracles of grace.
And keep them ever on my mind
that they may build my faith.
May I always see Your loving hand
in all that's good and kind.
And may I see it frequently
That You'll stay on my mind.
God, put me in over my head,
And make me know it's true.
When I succeed, there'll be no doubt,
the glory goes to You.
Amen

KAPoe

My Paltry Sacrifice

Please teach me how to praise You, Lord,
The way that You deserve.
My applause seems so unworthy
of the awesome God I serve.
The words I say can't be enough
to honor such a God.
How can a lowly wretch like me
lift Him Who I applaud?
So I bring my broken, contrite heart
for all the love You've shown.
I bring my broken spirit too
And lay them at Your throne.
To these I add obedience
in all You bid I do.
This is the paltry sacrifice
I dare to bring to You.
Because through faith I know Your grace
will give it greater worth.
Because of blood shed on the cross
that time You came to Earth.

Grace ✝ My Paltry Sacrifice

KAPoe

83

Feeding Jesus

ONE LOST SHEEP

The Lord appeared unto the Twelve
to show He'd cheated death,
To build their faith in Him alone,
And so, their lives to bless.
He didn't go to Peter.
Nor did He go to John.
He knew their love for Him was great.
He knew their faith was strong.
He's told us all, within the Word,
He'll leave the ninety nine
And go and search both high and low
The one lost sheep to find.
And so to Thomas He did go,
And said, "Now feel My hands.
And place your hand here in My side
that you may understand."
Throughout our lives He draws us near
and hopes that we will see
that He's the only path to God
for all eternity.

KAPoe

Feeding Jesus

THE DOCTOR IS IN

Because I lean on Jesus
some say He's just a crutch.
But He is so much more than that.
He heals with just a touch.
He is the Great Physician.
The Life Support. The Cure.
The only Medicine there is
for all that we endure.
He mends the lame so he can walk.
He makes the blind to see.
How can you say He's just a crutch?
You must be kidding me!
There is no wound that He can't mend.
He hardly leaves a scar.
He is the greatest X-ray Tech
and the finest Nurse by far.
So don't say He's just anything
But just a miracle.
He's so much more than just a crutch.
He's the whole Hospital.

Grace ✠ The Doctor Is In

KAPoe

85

THE STRONGEST MAN

The strongest Man Who ever lived
was good and kind and meek.
He fed the hungry, healed the lame,
and made the dumb to speak.
He carried weight none other can
And no one ever will.
He bore the load of every sin
and those we're making still.
Even Samson didn't have
the strength this Man has shown.
He couldn't bear all earthly sin.
He couldn't bear his own.
When Simon carried the cross that day,
a hefty weight he bore.
But Jesus carried to the cross
a weight that's so much more.

KAPoe

GRACE, AMAZING

God sent His Son into this world.
He watched as Jesus' life unfurled.
From town to town, on foot, He trod
to bring us messages from God.
Parables and wisdom from above
Meant to instill His brotherly love.
The people ran Him out of town.
Soldiers sent to track Him down.
They took the Lord we Christians hail,
beat Him, and threw Him in jail.
In a so called court they claimed His guilt.
They made Him carry the cross they'd built.
They took His garments and His shoes.
They spat upon the King of Jews.
The horrible way that they did treat Him,
Called Him names and kicked and beat Him.
On the cross our Lord was crucified.
Then a spear was stuck right through His side.
For three days Jesus Christ was dead
But on the third day raised His head.
For acts that should have brought damnation,
instead God's grace gave us salvation.

Grace ✝ Grace, Amazing

KAPoe

Feeding Jesus

KAPoe

Growth

Feeding Jesus

I Can See

Though I searched for life's essentials
They kept eluding me.
And though I knew they were close by,
My eyes just couldn't see.
I could sense it there in front of me.
And all things were in place.
Oh how I tried, but couldn't see
What's right before my face.
I prayed, "Dear God, please help me see
All things Your love will show.
I know there's much I really need
To see to thrive and grow."
Then slowly I began to see
A little more each day.
And God began to show me things
I need to live His way.
So silly, it was all right there.
It had been from the start.
These things the human eye can't see
You see them with your heart.

KAPoe

Feeding Jesus

I Shall Not Want

If you want what you can't have,
Or have what you don't want,
You open doors to discontent.
Your heart, these things will haunt.
Accept the things that you can't change,
But change the things you can.
In this you'll find contentment
To be a happy man.
Find the joy in what you have.
It's not so hard to do.
Embrace the gifts and promises
That God has given you.
If you seek your riches in His Word,
Great treasures He'll impart.
Wealth puts smiles on your face
But not upon your heart.
Some men who have great riches
And live in luxury
May never know the peace and joy
My Savior gives to me.

Growth ✠ I Shall Not Want

KAPoe

If God Permits

Put no faith in worldly things.
Only God knows what tomorrow brings.
You won't fulfill your future plans
Unless it's what God's will commands.
When you say, I promise it,
You should always say, if God permits.
It's all right to make your plans.
But be aware, they're in God's hands.
If you say I'll go, no matter what,
You just may find that door is shut.
Friendships then could be denied
If they perceive that you have lied.
We go forth on God's strength alone.
We accomplish nothing on our own.
If you've learned from this you've heard,
Praise God for giving me these words.

KAPoe

Feeding Jesus

FAMILY COUNSELING

Even the kings and presidents
Seek counsel from their staff.
Great wisdom and enlightenment
They share on his behalf.
Good counselors God sends to us,
His chosen family,
To guide us by His perfect Word
That they might help us see.
All honor comes from God alone
And not from worldly men.
And man's opinion matters not
When this life on Earth ends.
In multitudes of counselors
You're bound to find the way
To glorify God with your life
And do His will each day.
Employ the counsel of the saints.
Don't try to stand alone.
For when we work in harmony
Our love of God is shown.

KAPoe

FEAR

Convince yourself that wrong is good
Because some others say you should.
THAT IS FEAR.
Proclaim to all you know no fear
Because your friends might laugh or sneer.
THAT IS FEAR.
Pushing other people low
So your inadequacies won't show.
THAT IS FEAR.
You must stand taller than the rest.
You lie and cheat to be the best.
THAT IS FEAR.

Fear does not a coward make
Unless it owns the path you take.
Courage is not lack of fear.
It's standing firm when danger's near.
Each and every hero's made
By being brave though they're afraid.

When a man admits that he has fears,
His truthfulness admire.
But he who claims he has no fears
Is a fool or a liar.

Growth ✠ Fear

KAPoe

Feeding Jesus

FEELINGS

Many years ago I said
I never more would cry.
"No feelings that I ever have
will I let wet my eye.
I'll refuse to show emotion.
No one will foil my plan.
The world will see that I'm not weak.
I'll prove that I'm a man."
Then I let Jesus in my life.
And from the very start,
He changed the way I feel and think.
He gave me a new heart.
Though I'm still tough in trials I face,
my heart's not made of stone.
And I feel other people's pain
much deeper than my own.
I don't care what the world may think.
I'm not afraid to die.
Because of strength my Savior gives
I'm man enough to cry.

KAPoe

FROM THE HEART

How powerful the tongue can be.
It's made and toppled nations.
It's been the cause of many wars
Without exaggeration.
Tongues bring to light all evilness
contained within the heart.
Tongues are to blame for many tears
and families torn apart.
It starts within the heart and mind,
where hate and anger hide.
But pray to God to change your heart.
Those feelings will subside.
When love replaces all that hate,
at first it may seem strange.
The kind words you'll begin to speak
will be a welcome change.
A tongue is just as powerful
when used to spread God's love.
It can convince a sinner lost
to seek the Lord above.

Growth ✚ From The Heart

KAPoe

97

Feeding Jesus

KAPoe

GLORIFIED

May I glorify You, Lord, each day
By all I think and do and say.
Let not me to be anger moved
That You, within my heart, be proved.
May I lift You up, my Lord,
With my each and every word.
May some kindness I impart
Endear my God to someone's heart.
My thoughts be guided by Your will.
Your truth, within my mind, instill.
Please help me live Your Word each day
For mercies that I can't repay.
While shunning sin and hate and pride
That my Lord God be glorified.

Growth ✠ Glorified

Feeding Jesus

GOD CHANGES YOU

Why do folks try to find themselves?
You're nothing on your own.
Don't worry who you are inside
But how the Lord is shown.
The one you seek has died to sin,
Forever cast away.
And you can't know who you are now.
God changes you each day.
Don't concentrate on who you are
But who you hope to be.
Just let God change you from inside
For all eternity.
And when that happens, you won't care
Just who or what you were.
Through grace you'll emulate the Lord.
Of that you can be sure.
So keep your eyes upon the prize
Your ears upon the Lord.
Who you were will matter not
When you reach your reward.

KAPoe

Got A Light?

You can't take away the darkness
Without a source of light.
You can't take away your wrongness
Unless the Savior makes it right.
I read my Bible in the darkness.
With a little light I see.
But a little darkness in the light
Can't take my sight from me.
Absence of light is darkness,
Not the other way around.
There's no absence of darkness
Unless first the light is found.
You can't shine a beam of darkness
Through any place that's bright.
But His Light guides me undaunted
Right through the darkest night.

KAPoe

HE KNOWS

Our Father is a God of truth.
He will not hear the lies.
There's no forgiveness for the sin
A rebellious heart denies.
His heart wants to forgive you
As a father does his child.
Your truthfulness will set you free.
He will not be beguiled.
There's nothing that He doesn't know.
Admit to Him your crime.
Deceit will get you nowhere.
It's just a waste of time.
If you don't admit it to yourself,
Then you cannot confess it,
And of that sin you won't repent,
So how can God address it?
Maybe you don't know the truth.
Then find it in God's Word.
And then you'll know what you must do
So your prayers may be heard.

KAPoe

HEART TO HEART

If you are in a marriage
To a woman, man, or Christ,
Please give me just a moment,
And I'll give you some advice.
Be stronger in the hard times.
Be there to do your part.
Your time and effort given
Reflects what's in your heart.
Conversation is the key
When working as a team.
Only when you're heart to heart
United is your dream.
When the world crumbles around you,
Don't turn on those you love,
The ones who want to comfort you
And help you rise above.
Together, faithful, side by side,
Just bow your heads and pray.
Our loving God provides the Light
To guide you day by day.
Respect your holy union.
The two become as one.
The bonds you make through faithful love
Can never be undone.

KAPoe

Feeding Jesus

HERE I COME

I'm walking in His footsteps,
though my feet don't fill the mark.
And I'm leaping every step,
For they're so far apart.
So I ask the Lord, "Forgive me."
I know He understands.
My steps can't trace exactly
such a giant of a Man.
My steps will not be perfect
as the ones He left to show.
But with perseverance and His help
I'll follow where they go.
I do this not to live forever,
For I'm already saved.
I'm just following with all my heart
the example that He gave.

KAPoe

HIDDEN TREASURES

There are treasures in the Bible.
They're hidden in each book.
And you can reap great riches
If you will only look.
Wisdom is a treasure
Worth more than gold or gems.
For in it lies the answers
To all of life's problems.
Money may make you happy,
But once it's spent, it's gone.
Wisdom is a bank account
You can always draw upon.
Some say the road to happiness
Is wealth, no doubt about it.
But I'd trade it for the Word of God
And be happier without it.

KAPoe

Feeding Jesus

His House

When you let Jesus in your house
He'll want to give His best.
But He must be the master there.
He can't just be a guest.
You'll have to give your house to Him,
So sign away the deed.
It doesn't matter anyway.
He'll meet your every need.
He may want you to move some things.
Some other things can stay.
He'll help you clean your closets out
And throw some things away.
He'll paint no walls before they're fixed,
The way they ought to be.
For paint alone would be a lie
Meant for the world to see.
And floor by floor, He'll clean each room,
Removing filth and smell.
And when He's done your house will be
A place where He can dwell.

KAPoe

BREAK THE CHAIN

This steel chain is hard and strong,
Each link forged by the last.
Each link established in the chain
Perpetuates the past.
The pain and trials are past along.
Their acts and words degrade.
Each generation follows suit,
And so a chain is made.
Are you building another link
That's learning all your pain?
Then pray to God, it's not too late
For you to break the chain.
Don't let your legacy be pain
And insults that you've heard.
But start a legacy of love
That's guided by God's Word.
The legacy you start this day
Will praise God many fold.
So if you're going to build a chain
Then build a chain of gold.

KAPoe

Feeding Jesus

KAPoe

Feeding Jesus

Hand Of God

Feeding Jesus

KAPoe

GOD'S WAR

God says "we're sons of Abraham"
because we're sons of His.
And so we rest beneath His wings.
No safer place there is.
The devil hates God's chosen ones.
Our enemies abound.
So in the midst of many foes
will God's elect be found.
But we'll stand firm with courage.
We need not shield or sword.
With praise and worship we are armed.
The battle is the Lord's.
He turns our foes upon our foes,
Unstable in their ways.
With victory the Lord rewards
the warrior who prays.
And so the Lord is glorified,
Exalted by His saints.
Soon all the world will fear His name,
The God Who never faints.

KAPoe

City On A Hill

There was a city on a hill,
It's buildings tall and stout.
Into the darkness of the land
it's Light shown round about.
The leaders of the darkened land
despised the land of Light.
For it exposed their evil ways
and gave the people sight.
So they convinced the people there
the pure, sweet Light was bad.
They claimed it was an iron fist
and made the people mad.
Two thousand years, ten billion rocks,
the land of dark has thrown.
The city builds upon the rocks,
and how the city's grown.
They still throw rocks to quench the Light.
Through all, the city's stood.
The rocks they've thrown to cast it down
the Lord has used for good.

KAPoe

THE SANDSTORM

There were some thirty soldiers
who knew the dregs of war.
Ignoring human thoughts of fear,
they crossed the desert floor.
They traveled now by dark of night,
Their mission so covert.
They sought to rescue soldiers, brave,
the enemy had hurt.
A sandstorm came up suddenly.
It completely blocked their sight.
It stopped them right there in their tracks
and lasted through the night.
And so the soldiers knelt as one.
"We pray, God, it's Your will.
Please send Your Son to tame the wind
And tell it, "Peace, be still."
But through the night the wind blew on,
as though it were God's wrath.
Dawn's light showed that the wind exposed
the land mines in their path.

AMATUERS

With all the wisdom of the world
a mighty ship was made.
They called upon the wisest men
they found from every trade.
Professionals from all around
each worked their special skill.
The greatest vessel in the world
skilled laborers did build.
When finally done, the world was awed.
Magnificent was she.
They sold their tickets to the crowd
and put her out to sea.
To celebrate the victory
they feasted, sang, and drank.
But on the maiden voyage there
the great Titanic sank.
But when God sought to build an ark,
His deluge to endure,
God didn't seek the wisest men.
The Lord used amateurs.

I'M AN ARK

I'm just a lowly piece of wood,
No beauty on my own.
Unworthy of the love and grace
my holy God has shown.
He took me from the wilderness,
Into a box He formed me.
With pure, sweet gold, inside and out,
My Father then adorned me.
Protected by His cherubim,
Within their claws they clutch me.
And on my sides, poles clothed in gold,
that evil hands won't touch me.
The golden mercy seat of God
forever rests above me.
Reminding me that, through His grace,
my God will always love me.
I know that when the time is right
my eyes will see His face.
Till then He keeps me in His heart.
That's His most holy place.

KAPoe

Feeding Jesus

My Puzzle

Our childhood gives us pieces
of a puzzle, so to speak.
Then we hope they'll form a picture
of the happy life we seek.
But I was tossed from home to home,
Collecting pieces from each one.
So they didn't fit together,
And my puzzle can't be done.
The pieces formed an awful mess,
Confused and full of strife.
And so that mess became my guide
on how to live my life.
In time I said, "I can't go on,"
And to the Lord I cried.
He took the pieces from my hand,
and said, " I'll be your guide."
He spread His Word before my eyes,
and said, "Begin your search
For all life's wisdom lies within.
On this I've built My Church."

KAPoe

ZIG ZAGGING

Ordeals that we face in life
are turns along the way.
They make us walk a zig-zag path
that leads us to this day.
Each choice we make, each thing we do,
and all that we endure
creates a map that points us to
the present, true and sure.
The path I've walked was full of pain
and loneliness and strife.
So on a dark and angry road
I walked along in life.
But then that road led to the Lord,
no matter how I turned.
My heart was now prepared to hear
because of all I'd learned.
He took the anger from my heart
and made me want to sing.
So when I look into my past,
I wouldn't change a thing.

KAPoe

Feeding Jesus

BEAUTY FOR ASHES

God giveth and God takes away.
Don't let your joy grow dim.
For everything He gives or takes,
in truth, belongs to him.
There is no situation
nor evil Satan's tried
that God can't use, combined with grace,
that He'll be glorified.
No one on Earth has suffered
as the One that He begat.
See past the horror and the shame
the good that's come from that.
God gives water from a rock
and life from dried out bone.
He won't forsake us in our need.
We never stand alone.
Our God will comfort those who mourn,
that hearts be not cast down.
And from our ashes in His hand
He'll make a lovely crown.

KAPoe

BEHIND THE CURTAIN

Behind the curtain, constant banging.
Harder, softer, harder still.
Hammering relentlessly.
Oh, what can such noise fulfill?
Tossing, turning, rarely sleeping,
as the racket lingers on.
Tears and rage well up inside me
through the constant evil song.
Why must I suffer for no reason?
What good can come of this I hear?
I think that soon I may go crazy.
I hate this pounding in my ears.
Daily, nightly, sound unending.
I can't take it, and I crack.
In a rage I grab the curtain,
and, in anger, yank it back.
In awe and wonder stands my True Love.
Hammer, chisel, tight in hand.
Amidst the rubble, awesome beauty.
There a lovely statue stands.

ACCIDENTAL MASS PERFECTION?

Our God created all we see
of sky and sea and land.
Just like a Mighty Artist,
with holy brush in hand.
He painted man and beast and tree,
Each flower in the field.
And with one graceful, flowing stroke,
the moon and stars revealed.
He painted every mountain scape,
Each lake and valley too.
And every dawn and sunset
that man will ever view.
There are those who'll try to tell you
it's all an accident.
Some paint just spilled and made this mess
Without design, thought, or intent.
I'm fighting to compose myself.
Dear Lord, lend me Your grace.
For I know it won't be Christian like
to laugh before their face.

KAPoe

EAGLES

In Jesus, I'm an eagle
in flight forever more.
Because His love is limitless,
eternally I soar.
The Spirit is a godly breeze
that lifts beneath my wings.
He carries me so high above
that I might see all things.
In faith, I glide upon the wind,
relying on His power.
But if I flapped my wings in vain,
I wouldn't last an hour.
I teach the little ones to fly,
And pray they'll leave the nest,
to hunt the meat within the Word
That they might pass each test.
Within the Light He shines by day,
such joy my Savior brings.
And through the night times of my life
I'll rest beneath His wings.

Feeding Jesus

KAPoe

Feeding Jesus

Leadership

Feeding Jesus

KAPoe

Feeding Jesus

SHEPHERDS

God sends a shepherd for each flock
with rod and staff in hand.
In love he shows them where to graze
the best fields in the land.
In time, he knows each one by name.
They follow him by choice.
He speaks the Word and all will come
because they know his voice.
In Jesus' name he slays the bears
and wolves that seek them out.
And by God's grace he takes the lamb
right from the lion's mouth.
He speaks the truth in gentle tones
and says the things he must.
And so they are not prone to stray
because he's earned their trust.
He calls the blemished, vain, and proud
and leads them to the Lord.
And if they hearken to his voice,
God's grace is their reward.

FATHER'S STRENGTH

A good Dad is a man of strength.
He's strong enough to love.
In strength, he puts himself aside
to follow God above.
His greatest strength is character.
He's strong enough to bend.
His hands can gently hold a babe
And yet his house defend.
He shows his family how to live.
Example is the key.
So through the wisdom of the Word
he guides them on his knees.
His compassion is not weakness.
It's a virtue God imparts.
He breaks his child's stubborn ways
But doesn't break his heart.
He's faithful, and he's humble.
His love none can deny.
And when his children come to Christ,
he's strong enough to cry.

KAPoe

WAYWARD

The Father sits upon the roof,
searching the horizon.
He cries so many tears each day.
He's waiting for His son.
His son has packed and gone away,
Some happiness to find,
Forgetting all the broken hearts
at home he's left behind.
He's built a wall around his heart.
Their love can't penetrate.
And so they reach out to the Lord.
And in their tears they wait.
The little ones don't understand.
They ask their mother, "Please,
tell me what's in Daddy's heart
that he loves more than me?"
How can the mother tell the child,
through pain of heart that stings,
his heart cries out for something bad,
And death is all it brings.
And so in tears the child prays,
through sobs that take the breath,
"Please make of me the kind of child
my Dad loves more than death."

KAPoe

Feeding Jesus

Feeding Jesus

Obedience

Feeding Jesus

The Godly Man

Righteousness and godliness
are really not the same.
For righteousness is but a gift
God gives in Jesus' name.
It is the absence of all sin
the Father takes away.
Then through His mercy and His love
He cleanses us each day.
But godliness is not a gift.
It's how we choose to live.
It's how we treat our neighbor
and how we choose to give.
Our Father God is holy.
He says, "Be holy too,
and follow Christ's example
in everything you do."
God made us in His image.
We're perfect in His eyes.
He told us this in His sweet Word.
But lack of faith denies.
So live a life that's holy,
and follow Jesus' plan.
When you forgive, love, teach, and serve,
then you're a godly man.

KAPoe

Right Side Up

Sometimes God puts things on my heart
that I think sound insane.
They make no earthly sense at all
inside my finite brain.
He's patient if I doubt it's Him.
No answer if I pray.
Except to get my Bible out
and see if it's His way.
I search for any pros or cons
to guide the choice I make.
Then, if it's true, I look for ways
to guide the steps I take.
Sometimes I still don't think it's wise.
It's upside down to me.
God's wisdom is so wonderful
sometimes we just can't see.
But I step out in obedience
because I love the Lord.
And soon the crazy thing I do
brings my heart grand reward.

KAPoe

Feeding Jesus

THE PROMISE

When a man thought all was hopeless
and that he'd surely die,
with all his heart and mind and strength
unto the Lord he cried.
I know that I'm a sinner, God.
I know I've been untrue.
But I promise, if You save my life,
then I'll give it to You.
And so the Father spared his life.
He strove to serve God more.
But he only served with all his heart
behind the prison door.
Then, when released, he'd soon neglect
his promise to the Lord.
He left his Bible at the gate
to seek worldly reward.
Now serving life without parole,
he prays, "God, set me free.
I feel that I've been cast away,
and You've forsaken me."
God said, "IN LOVE, I'VE PLACED YOU THERE,
THIS WORLD'S REWARDS TO FADE.
IT'S WHERE YOU NEED TO BE TO KEEP
THE PROMISE THAT YOU MADE."

Obedience ✚ The Promise

KAPoe

133

GRAY AREAS

There are some areas in life
I chose to justify.
And through the grace bought on the cross
I've spread my wings to fly.
I had interpreted God's Word
by what made sense to me.
Although good Christians disagreed,
my eyes refused to see.
And so I challenged them to use
God's Word to prove me wrong.
I said they'd twisted God's good Word
to make their case seem strong.
So I determined they're unwise.
They proved nothing to me.
I guessed that meant that I had won.
I claimed the victory.
God said, "Before you tell all men
you're righteous in your sight,
I challenge you to use My Word
to prove to Me you're right."
The truth was that I didn't know
if it was good or bad.
And so I cannot take the chance
my acts could make God sad.

KAPoe

Feeding Jesus

ZEALOTS

Do you jump up and yell real loud
When some lost soul gets saved?
Have you rejoiced and clapped your hands
For each new life God gave?
Does your heart race and your palms sweat
For family members new?
Do you go out and tell your friends
Just what it means to you?
And when that soul is then baptized,
Do your feet leave the ground?
The way they will if your best team
Should make that last touchdown?
If your heart truly loves the Lord
And treasures each command,
Those victories should make you show
The zeal of a fan.

Obedience ✠ Zealots

KAPoe

Feeding Jesus

His

The Lord said, "It is finished."
Salvation's work was done.
Then His Spirit left the body
that on the cross was hung.
We work because we love the Lord.
Our life and body's His.
Because He gave the same for us,
No greater love there is.
And so we must lay down our lives
in honor of His death.
Because He bought us with a price,
He owns our every breath.
We cannot earn His love or grace.
We earn a lovely crown.
Someday we'll take it to His throne,
and there we'll lay it down.
So we must plant His seed in faith
in this parched and barren place,
That in His time and will and love
a rose may grow through grace.

Obedience ✚ His

KAPoe

THE GREATEST TEST

Money is the greatest test
that God has given man.
Will we choose it over faithfulness
or love or God's commands?
For love of money man will steal
and cheat, deceive and hide.
And then for his ill gotten gain
he'll puff his chest in pride.
We pray, "God bring prosperity."
We know it's His to give.
And so He blesses us with much
of what we need to live.
There're always ways to spend it all.
We see less than there is.
And so, in greed, withhold our tithes,
Forgetting that it's His.
If you believe there is a Heaven,
Then build your treasures there.
Or there'll be many empty rooms
in the house that God prepares.

Feeding Jesus

All She Has

A poor old woman once there was,
Her husband long since dead.
She worked her fingers to the bone
to keep her family fed.
She labored for each meal they ate.
And daily did she strive
to scant produce what they need most
and keep them all alive.
No Bible did she ever own.
But from sermons that she'd heard,
though sometimes they'd no food to eat,
she fed them with the Word.
She early rose each Sabbath morn,
And walking while she'd sing,
she'd walk a mile in worn out shoes
To make her offering.
She didn't stop to think of what
tomorrow held in store.
Through tears she prayed, "I love You, God.
I wish I could give more."
A rich man, showing his disdain
and overflowing pride,
laughed when he saw the woman put
her last two cents inside.

KAPoe

Feeding Jesus

Each week she gives all that she has
because she loves the Lord.
And since she gives all from the heart
she earns a grand reward.

Obedience ✝ All She Has

Feeding Jesus

ANY MOMENT

He could show up any moment,
Unexpected as a thief.
God only knows exactly when.
Our time here could be brief.
What is it you'll be doing
When He comes upon the cloud?
Will you be ashamed to see Him?
Or will you make Him proud?
Will it be the very moment
That the tempter draws you in?
Then in the twinkling of an eye
He'll find you in your sin.
We must live every moment
As though it were the one
The trumpet blast will fill the air
And we will meet God's Son.
Be constant in the Savior's work
Until He intervenes.
And that is how He'll find you.
That's what "BE READY" means.

KAPoe

CHECK YOURSELF

Some quote the Bible all the day
For all the world to hear,
While hiding prejudice and hate
And feigning love and cheer.
They may fool some but not the Lord.
All truth comes to His eyes.
They twist God's words to plead their case
And turn them into lies.
They pose as saints for all to see.
Their hearts are far away.
They puff their chest and walk in pride
Until the judgment day.
Let's join as one and pray for them
Before it is too late.
God, let their hardened hearts to yield
Before they seal their fate.
If you're upset by this you read
Then look at no one else.
The truth lies heavy on your heart.
You need to check yourself.

KAPoe

ENLISTED MAN

Dear Lord, You are the reason now
For everything I do.
Because You are the reason that
I choose to see life through.
All the hopes and dreams I have
Are hinged upon my faith
That You will keep Your promises
Through Your abounding grace.
I know You're real and great and true.
I'm answering Your call.
For if I'm wrong, it's all absurd.
We've no purpose at all.
I know of Your great love for me.
What I didn't know was why.
I never sought to please my God.
I didn't even try.
Those days are gone. You've changed my heart.
And now I understand.
So I will waste this life no more.
I place it in Your hands.
Suddenly I've sight and gifts
I've never known before.
They're mighty weapons in my hand
When fighting for the Lord.

KAPoe

Feeding Jesus

No matter what You call me for,
Your Word will be obeyed.
With confidence that You'll smile upon
This soldier that You've made.

EVERY EFFORT

You're not really just a clay pot
But something much, much more.
You weren't made on the wheel.
That's just a metaphor.
God doesn't mold you with His hands.
He shapes you with His Word.
He prompts you with His Spirit,
That still, small voice you've heard.
It's true that like a lump of clay
You're nothing on your own.
But in you dwells the Spirit.
That means you're not alone.
You can't just simply sit there
And let God do it all.
You must make every effort
To answer His great call.
Don't ever get discouraged,
But do all that you can
To live a life that's holy.
For that's the Father's plan.

KAPoe

A BETTER HOST

The Holy Spirit's in your heart.
He shares your life with you.
And every day He's in the midst
Of everything you do.
When you conform unto this world,
Subjecting Him to wrong,
You put those headphones on His ears
To hear that filthy song.
He's there with you at TV time
To watch those violent scenes.
And you subject Him to your lust
For girls in magazines.
So try to be a better host
To your invited Guest.
And through renewal of your mind,
He'll help you be your best.
Don't quench the Spirit of the Lord.
Do what He says you should.
And prove the perfect will of God
Acceptable and good.

KAPoe

FIRED UP

There is a fire in my soul
That burns for my dear Lord,
A fire burning far too bright
To ever be ignored.
The fire of God is always good.
It tests and purifies.
So those who love Him need not fear.
Only the evil dies.
May my works not "stubble" be
When tested by the fire.
May selfishness not be the fuel
That feeds my heart's desire.
May my heart be His burning bush,
An unconsuming flame.
And may I hear and do His will
In reverence to His name.
The judgment day will bring the test
Of faith none can pretend.
So if your soul burns not for Him,
It may burn in the end.

Obedience ✚ Fired Up

KAPoe

Follow Me

Each day I must take up my cross
And walk to Calvary.
I sacrifice myself for Him,
A servant for to be.
My old self must be crucified.
I die to sin each day.
If I'm to walk as Jesus walked,
Then that's the only way.
He's with me on the road each day
To guide me patiently.
He says, "I'VE WALKED THIS ROAD BEFORE.
YOU NEED JUST FOLLOW ME."
If I will give my life to Him,
He'll give it back to me.
I trade the worthless for the best
And live eternally.
The precious gold we love on Earth,
And hoard in our abodes,
Cannot compare to Heaven's best.
It's used to pave the roads.

KAPoe

GREEN BRANCHES

Don't make a bad impression.
You represent the Lord.
If He gets blamed for what you do,
You lead them from reward.
When Christians act like righteous snobs,
Submerged in vain conceit,
They're doomed to walk in fruitlessness.
Their witness they defeat.
Our Savior told the Pharisees
To serve and humble be.
A lesson meant not just for them,
He spoke for you and me.
So try to be like Jesus Christ
In all you say and do.
And when they see Him in your heart,
They'll want to know Him too.
And so you'll be a lush green branch
That from the vine did shoot,
Through which His righteous juices flow
That you may bear much fruit.

KAPoe

I Have Purpose

My mouth's agape in disbelief.
The sensation feels so odd.
I just realized a wretch like me
Can help our awesome God.
I'm going to pay my tithes in full,
A gift that I afford.
Giving up vain things I want
To glorify the Lord.
The ones that He leads me to help
May praise Him for His grace.
That possibility will keep a smile
Ever growing on my face.
I'm overjoyed, I've finally found
The purpose I've searched for.
I am a faithful servant now.
What man could ask for more?

KAPoe

I'm A Hammer

I esteem myself not good nor bad
nor worthy as I am,
Except when I am wielded
by my Creator's hand.
I'm just His tool on a shelf
awaiting my next task.
Available for any work,
He needn't even ask.
Because I am within His hand,
the work I do won't fail.
I know He's guiding me aright
each time I meet the nail.
I sink each nail in His time.
I feel no pride nor guilt.
It's not important if I see
the lovely house that's built.
The nail that's in front of me
is what's important now.
The skill I lack does matter not
Because my God knows how.

Obedience ✚ I'm A Hammer

KAPoe

Use Me

One day while riding on a bus
I bowed my head to pray.
"I thank You Father for Your love.
Please use Your child today."
Just then a man got on the bus
And sauntered down the aisle.
The largest man I'd ever seen.
I tried to force a smile.
His arms were bigger than my legs.
Eyes locked in steely stare.
He sat down right across from me.
He filled the double chair.
I heard a small voice in my head
Say, "Give that man a tract."
My eyes got big, my mouth agape,
But I did not react.
"You said, Please use me, so get up
And do this thing I say.
Just love thy neighbor as thyself.
Reach out to him today."
I fought the fear that held me back.
And in the Father's strength,
I fumbled for a random tract
And held it out at length.

KAPoe

Feeding Jesus

He took the tract and read it through.
A tear ran down his cheek.
He held the tract up to his chest
And he began to speak.
He sobbed, "I'd like to thank you friend
For reaching out today.
These are the very words I need
To help me on my way."

Obedience ✚ Use Me

KAPoe

Feeding Jesus

Overcoming

Overcoming ✝ Contents

KAPoe

Feeding Jesus

DON'T FEED THE BEAST

There was a man who fed a beast.
He did it just for fun.
But then he kept on feeding it
until it weighed a ton.
The beast he'd innocently fed
now brings him pain and strife.
And now it tells him what to do,
A monster in his life.
He prayed, "Dear God, I need Your help.
This thing's too big for me.
Please tame this Monster in my life,
and I will follow Thee."
God put the monster in a cage
and closed the iron door.
He said, "THIS BEAST CAN'T HARM YOU NOW.
DON'T FEED IT ANY MORE."
So, day by day, the man obeyed.
He starved it for awhile.
The man said, "It's no monster now,"
But he was in denial.
A serpent spoke unto the man.
He said, "The cage is strong.
If you fed him, just a tiny bit,

KAPoe

Feeding Jesus

the beast could do no wrong.
The beast is weak, it's in a cage,
and it will be all right."
And so, in time, the man gave in
and gave the beast a bite.
When all went well, the man got brave
and fed it more and more.
In time the beast became so strong,
it broke the iron door.
Again the beast reigned in his life,
tormenting all his days.
Again the man prayed, "God, please help,
and I will change my ways."
Again the Lord was merciful.
Again God caged the beast.
This time the man stayed on his knees,
and soon his anguish ceased.
The man rebukes the serpent now.
This time the devil lost.
The weakened beast sits in his cage.
The cage sits at the cross.

KAPoe

THE SUITCASE

There is a suitcase in my hand.
It's filled with rocks and chains.
They are the weight from my life's trials
that in my heart remains.
It hinders all I try to do.
It makes me slow and weak.
It is a wall that keeps me from
the purpose that I seek.
And so one day I closed my eyes.
I bowed my head and prayed.
"Dear Lord, won't You have mercy
on this creature that You've made?"
I felt something inside my heart
that overcame my strife.
God said, "Enter the water,
and I will change your life."
"But God, this heavy burden
is sure to weigh me down.
If I go into the water,
I'm sure that I will drown."
God said, "By your own understanding
you accumulate that weight.
And it's by what you think you know
that you might seal your fate.

KAPoe

Feeding Jesus

You stand before Me broken,
with that suitcase in your hand.
You put that weight in there yourself,
But that was not My plan.
There was a lesson in your trials
for you to learn and grow.
But instead of learning something new,
you trusted what you know.
This world is but a tiny speck,
A pebble in the sea.
But it is all you'll ever know
unless you follow Me.
There is no limit of My love
and mercy to receive.
Just spurn the wisdom of this world
and let your heart believe."
So, with my suitcase in my hand
I walked into the sea.
I said, "Please take me as I am,
and I will follow Thee."
The suitcase that had held me down
began to bob and float.
The trials that I had faced in life
had now become my boat.

KAPoe

Jesus School

I said, "It's not that easy, God,
to just let my past go."
He smiled at me with teary eyes.
And then God said, "I know."
"My heart pounds fiercely in my chest.
My pain and fury grow."
He reached His strong arms out to me.
And then God said, "I know."
He said, "I do know how you feel.
Your pain is real and true.
But do you know that's Satan's voice
that keeps reminding you?
He fills your head with hateful lies.
He tells you you're to blame.
He tells you that you're on your own
to wallow in your shame.
Please dry your eyes and listen, child.
It's time for Jesus school.
Next time the devil speaks his lies,
you tell him, Shut up, fool!
And then say, Jesus is my strength.
In Him my spirit sings.
Don't tell me I can't overcome.
In Him I do all things."

KAPoe

DIRTY BUSINESS

The devil's in the business
of leading us astray
And keeping others in the dark
so they can't find the way.
He has declared a war on Earth.
He's trained his army well.
His goal: Divide and conquer,
That more might go to Hell.
He plants his seeds within the church,
and arguments ensue.
And churches are divided.
The one becomes the two.
So many doctrines follow Christ.
They claim the only way.
They love their doctrines more than Christ
and all He had to say.
He said to keep the peace in love.
He said to reconcile.
Disunity among the church
is making Satan smile.

KAPoe

HARD TIMES

I thank You for the mountains, God,
that You've made me to climb.
I thank You for the doors You've closed
until it was my time.
I thank You for my hungry days
that give me empathy.
I thank You for the wisdom gained
through Your chastising me.
It was the hard times in my life,
the days which I had spurned,
that You have used to teach me, Lord,
And through them I have learned.
So I thank You for the sad times
that You let me go through.
The more of them that I endure
the more I am like You.
Please help me to remember, God,
whenever I'm in pain,
You always have a reason, Lord.
I suffer not in vain.

Overcoming ✝ Hard Times

KAPoe

Feeding Jesus

CONFIDENCE

Lord, help me come with confidence
that Your grace has overcome
the dark paths I have walked in life
and wrong things I have done.
Please help me to get past the fact
that no man can deserve
the blessings that flow freely from
the awesome God I serve.
I ask You for prosperity.
But put it on my heart
to share with others, who have need,
the gift that You impart.
I come to You in righteousness.
But it is not my own.
It is a gift that You bestow
on those knelt at Your throne.
Please help me come with confidence
to You, my God above,
that You take joy in giving gifts
to those whose faith You love.

KAPoe

CONQUER

Zacchaeus didn't say, "I'm short,"
and simply walk away.
The blind man didn't hold his tongue
at the crowd's rebuke that day.
Paul didn't say, "I can't go on
with this thorn in my side."
And Jacob said, "I won't let go
until I'm blessed." He cried.
Don't give up or say, "I can't,"
to opportunity.
Don't let your guiding force be fear
or insecurity.
We're more than conquerors in Christ.
We must believe it's true.
For He's the wisdom, strength, and drive
to do what we must do.
Don't listen to the evil one,
who speaks defeat and shame.
God's hand supports His faithful ones
who step out in His name.

KAPoe

Feeding Jesus

FORGED BY FIRE

I was born into adversity,
Abused and cast away.
Each hour was a separate hell
I lived through day by day.
Raised by strangers without love;
A freak among my peers;
Confused and lonely in the world;
As such I spent my years.
So I became the things I hate,
My pain and rage to share.
But no joy came in my revenge
Because, somehow, I cared.
I shook my tongue and fist at God.
I said, "What God are You?
How can You sit there on Your throne
and watch what I go through?"
God said, "Those trials were needed.
That pain you had to feel.
Because it takes a mighty fire
to forge and strengthen steel.
I've loved you, though I've hated
the things you've felt and done.
But I will use those things for good
when you become My son.

164   KAPoe

Feeding Jesus

Peace

Peace ✚ Contents

Feeding Jesus

KAPoe

GIVE ME PEACE

Lord, give me peace instead of strife
when things don't go my way in life.
When other folks dishonor me
may my heart know serenity.
Let this not be a stumbling block
that trips me up along my walk.
Help me forgive the things they've said
That it won't stain my heart or head.
And when my hurts and woes compile,
walk with me on that extra mile.
May compassion fill the words I speak
that I'll show the mercy that I seek.
Let love and faithfulness instill
my earnest quest to do Your will.
Please give me not what I won't give.
May Your Light shine through how I live.
Forgive my sins, no less nor better,
Than just as I forgive my debtors.

Amen

Feeding Jesus

PEACE IN THE STORM

*P*ray God will give you strength to claim
the peace, Christ said, "I leave you."
And trials you face can't cancel it.
And your heart won't deceive you.

*E*ndure the storms with hope and faith,
And let the tempest teach you.
For Jesus stands upon the waves,
And, in God's time, He'll reach you.

*A*ccept God's wisdom when doors close
or rocky paths impede us.
For when our hearts are calm and still,
our Savior's voice will lead us.

*C*all out to God, in Jesus' name,
His promises abounding.
His joy is always yours to claim
in spite of vain surroundings.

*E*ncourage others as you go,
in grace to face the test.
In rage, our pain and anguish reign.
In peace, we know God's rest.

KAPoe

Feeding Jesus

Persecution

Persecution ✝ Contents

Feeding Jesus

KAPoe

EXPOSED

Wickedness hates righteousness.
For good exposes sin.
And evil's ugly face is shown
By its comparison.
So it rebukes morality
And decency and virtue.
It tries to make you feel inept
And says mean things to hurt you.
It ignores the laws of God and man
Because it can't respect it.
It claims there is no punishment
If man doesn't detect it.
It says there is no afterlife.
It's all a fantasy.
The fact is it wants not to change.
It's what it wants to be.
So just by living in God's will,
We expose it to the rest.
And so we plant abundant seed
By giving God our best.

KAPoe

Feeding Jesus

KAPoe

Feeding Jesus

Perseverance

Feeding Jesus

THIS WILDERNESS

We don't step out of Egypt
into the Promised Land
But first into the wilderness
of hills and snakes and sand.
Our attitude will set the pace.
So through our woes and fears,
the short trek God intends for us
Might take us forty years.
Be thankful for the providence
God gives us day by day.
And don't deny the miracles
we see along the way.
It's not our giant enemies
that keep us from our goal.
Through lack of faith and grumbling,
God can't prepare our soul.
So many hear the promises.
Victorious are few.
Of all the men God led away,
the Promised Land saw two.

KAPoe

My Little Cross

My little cross cannot compare
to that which Jesus bore.
On my small cross I die to self
But Christ for so much more.
From our sins, deserving death,
our Savior set us free.
And for His perfect innocence
we hung Him on a tree.
It was His choice to suffer death
to cleanse us of our sin.
And so, by choice, we die to self
that we might live for Him.
If we believe, we must commit
to share His precious name.
Our reasons made to not comply
are meant to hide our shame.
So step out of your comfort zone,
just momentarily,
that you might lead a soul to Christ
for all eternity.

KAPoe

Feeding Jesus

TRIAL TREASURES

The songs we sing from mountain tops
are precious to God's ears.
But worship from the valleys low
can bring God joyful tears.
God uses trials in our lives
to shape and mold and form.
Then He's the Lighthouse on the rocks
that guides us through the storm.
It's hardships that prepare the way
to the kingdom up above.
God knows that they will make us strong.
He leads us there in love.
If, in this process we must bear,
we murmur in God's sight,
we'll surely face those trials again
Until we get it right.
Those times aren't there to hurt us
Though they grieve us for awhile.
What doesn't kill us makes us strong.
There's treasure in the trial.

KAPoe

Valley School

The deeper the valley
the higher the hill.
In the depth of the valley,
we learn the LORD's will.
We walk through the valley.
It's no place to run
or we'll miss the lesson.
No hill when we're done.
I hate not the valleys.
I walk with the Lord.
The wisdom I gain there
is God's sweet reward.
The journey's not easy.
Some valleys are long.
But it's through our trials
that God makes us strong.
Don't try to avoid them
For it's the Lord's will.
We learn in the valleys
and rest on the hills.

Perseverance ✝ Valley School

KAPoe

Feeding Jesus

Against The Flow

There will be those of hardened hearts
Whose hatred breeds contempt.
They will not hear my witnessing.
They'll stifle each attempt.
They'll point their finger, and they'll say
There's something wrong with me.
He confesses bold that he believes
In things the world can't see.
Other souls, through blindness,
With true concern might say
The path I walk's against the flow.
I'm going the wrong way.
What they perceive as normal
Is what the world believes.
Satan leads them blind into the pit.
Each heart his lie deceives.
Only God can grant them faith.
None else can meet their needs.
Just pray for them with diligence,
And keep on planting seeds.

KAPoe

All Aboard

I sit within my tiny boat
in the turmoil of the sea,
Rowing toward the destination
that the Lord appointed me.
Fighting waves of days gone by
and whirlpools of remorse,
The Spirit will provide the strength
to keep my boat on course.
Larger ships go racing by
and tip me in their wake.
But prayers and perseverance
keep me on the path I take.
Unforgiving ocean beasts
that bump me with their tails,
try to sink my tiny boat,
but righteousness prevails.
Other boats just like my own
attach themselves to me.
Together we endure the fury
of the wicked sea.
Collectively a mighty ship
of enormous length and girth.
Supernaturally withstanding
all the evils of this Earth.
Storms create gigantic waves

KAPoe

Feeding Jesus

that slap against our bow.
But easily we overcome.
for God's Word shows us how.
Our eyes on the horizon,
Searching for the golden glow
of the New Jerusalem
And the Lord we've come to know.
Then we'll live in peace and praise.
Our battle we'll have won.
Wrapped forever in the love and warmth
of God's most precious Son.

KAPoe

Bring It On

If the devil never bothers you,
He must not be upset.
If he's got better things to do,
You must not be a threat.
But the devil can't ignore me
Because I'm doing what I can
To spread the good news everywhere
And praise the Son of man.
When Satan tries to get my goat,
I tell him, "Bring it on.
If my God let's you test me,
He helps me to be strong."
When he tries to rile or tempt me,
I just pull out my Sword.
For when I quote the Scriptures,
I'm speaking for my Lord.
The devil hates to hear God's words.
They make him weak and small.
So though I suffer for a time,
I know that I won't fall.
Even in my darkest hours,
My Savior's Light I see.
So faithfully He shows the path
That leads to victory.

KAPoe

Feeding Jesus

CAN DO

A Christian who is Spirit filled
Is powered by the Lord,
A messenger of Father God
Who should not be ignored.
Boldness to enlightenment,
Though still maintaining meekness.
A God exalting humbleness
That fools mistake for weakness.
If you are living in His Word,
Then He will use you too.
The Spirit knows your heart and mind.
He knows what you can do.
Believe you can do all He says
With Words that never lie.
If lack of faith makes you say no,
The Father you deny.
And woe to those who hinder you
And try to block your path.
It's they who should be sore afraid
To know the Father's wrath.

KAPoe

ENDURE

Sometimes it's through our tears and woes
that Jesus' love most brightly shows.
Through grief a crowd becomes as one.
Through pain the Father's will is done.
Our scars in life we bear for others.
They make us wise to guide our brothers.
And through the sting of trials we learn
great wisdom we can share in turn.
It's those ordeals we endure
that make our testimony sure.
The time in anguish that we spend
becomes the bridge to help a friend.
Sometimes because of tests we shirk.
God can't prepare us for His work.
Endure the hardships and the loss.
And leave your worries at the cross.
Because all healing for all lands
all flows from Jesus' wounded hands.

Perseverance ✚ Endure

Feeding Jesus

FILTHY RAGS

When Jesus reached down in the mire
And grabbed a hold of you,
He stripped you of your filthy rags
And cleaned you through and through.
He took you in and gave you bread
And made your blind eyes see.
He loves you and He comforts you
And makes you family.
The gift of life He gives to you
And saves you from the fire.
And if your heart delights in God,
He grants your heart's desire.
But in this world, you'll still have tears.
Sometimes things may look dim.
Those are the times that test your faith.
You must believe in Him.
Don't let the bad times steal your joy.
Don't think His love has gone.
Don't throw yourself back in the mire
Or put the rags back on.

Perseverance ✚ Filthy Rags

KAPoe

Feeding Jesus

Praise

Praise ✠ Contents

Feeding Jesus

KAPoe

I Love You, Lord

I love You for Your mercy, Lord,
A gift I don't deserve.
I love You for Your faithfulness,
My God Who came to serve.
I love You for Your patience, Lord.
In loving tears You wait.
So long You watched me run amok
Then saved me from my fate.
You are the love I feel for You.
For more of You I thirst.
My heart and soul and life are Yours
Because You loved me first.
I love You for my life You gave.
You formed me in the womb.
And You knocked on my heart's door
to save my soul from doom.
I love You for Your sacrifice.
Because of You, I'm free.
How could my heart not so adore
the God Who died for me?

KAPoe

Feeding Jesus

In His Names

JESUS, SAVIOR from our shames,
May these words praise Your precious names.
SON OF GOD, EMMANUEL,
Who came to save our souls from hell.
From the mountain tops may You be heard.
Oh TEACHER of GOD and the WORD.
CHIEF CORNER STONE on God's foundation,
Help us build Your Christian nation.
ALPHA, OMEGA and all between,
We've faith in You though You're unseen.
The LAMB OF GOD, the ONE TRUE VINE,
Who promises no end of time.
Great MESSIAH, sweet REDEEMER,
Cleansing pure the lustful dreamer.
For the LORD OF LORDS and KING OF KINGS,
Let trumpets sound and angels sing.
We bless You, and we praise You, BROTHER.
For You're the WAY, and there's no other.

AMEN

Music To God's Ears

We laud our praise and worship team
Whose many gifts are shown.
They lead us all in heartfelt song
unto the Father's throne.
Each song, sweet voice, and instrument,
Each old and cherished hymn
is twice as sweet to God above
And beckons He come in.
His Spirit overfills the house
each week throughout the years.
Our praise and worship offering
is precious to His ears.
So raise your hands and sing out loud
to our dear Lord above.
That He might shed sweet tears of joy
because of our great love.

KAPoe

PLEASE DON'T CUT ME

I love God as I've never loved.
He loves me as none else.
He holds me higher in His heart
than I could hold myself.
He is my Father and my Friend
for all eternity.
And so He took on human form
so He could die for me.
I cannot tell you what to do,
and I won't even try.
God says that "everyone must choose"
where they go when they die.
Whether you believe or not,
why would you soil His name?
If you don't think that He exists,
your words are quite insane.
No man can comprehend His love.
I've given Him my life.
So when you use His name in vain,
it cuts me like a knife.

KAPoe

Prayer

Prayer ✚ Contents

Feeding Jesus

KAPoe

God Hears

The blood of Abel cried to God.
He heard it from the ground.
"Without revenge I cannot rest.
May justice soon be found."
And so the Father spoke to Cain,
Condemned him for his deed.
And God proclaimed a curse on him,
from which he'd not be freed.
The blood of Jesus cries to God.
He hears His Son's blood too.
"Have mercy on our enemies.
Let their faith make them new."
So God proclaims His grace on those
who come unto His Son.
"May peace and joy be in your hearts.
Your sins are now undone."
Have faith, the Father hears your prayers.
Right words His heart will flood.
No heartfelt prayer escapes the Lord.
He even hears the blood.

KAPoe

Feeding Jesus

HEART ACHES

Dear God, send me a Christian
whose heart and mind forgives.
Succumbing not to worldly views,
But by Your Word she lives.
She knows that we're all sinners,
But we're perfect in Your sight.
She seeks a man who loves You
with his heart and soul and might.
Let her see me in the present
By the fruit I bear today,
Not by the mire in my past,
My Father, God, I pray.
My heart aches for a Christian,
A sinner You've made new,
Whose tender heart receives and shares
the grace she's found in You.
Please lead our hearts together, God,
That I may end my search
at the hand of someone I can love
as Jesus loves the church.
Amen

KAPoe

FOR ALL YOU'VE DONE

For all the times you've prayed to God
To take me in His arms,
For every time you asked the Lord
To save my soul from harm,
I owe you far more than I did,
For all you've done for me.
Your prayers have brought me love and joy
For all eternity.
There's a special place within my heart
For the mother I admire.
You've saved me from eternal death
In Satan's lake of fire.

Prayer ✚ For All You've Done

Feeding Jesus

PRAY FOR ISRAEL

Those who curse God's chosen ones
will make that curse their own.
God promises that we will reap
exactly what we've sown.
If our nation sides with Palestine,
Don't join in with the rest.
For if we pray for Israel
our faithfulness is blessed.
The wicked march on Zion.
Don't follow in their path.
Or you will see just what it means
to know the Father's wrath.
But the faithful are protected.
We rest beneath God's wings,
Guarded from the pestilence
and plague God's anger brings.
Though a thousand fall right near you,
Ten thousand at your hand,
You'll only see the punishment
God brings upon the land.

KAPoe

*V*ICTORY

The thick, dark clouds, one sunny day,
were hidden well from me.
Because they were within a realm
that my eyes couldn't see.
Amidst the mighty thunder clash
the spirits waged their war.
The holy bodies fall like rain,
So God sends in some more.
The evil one abounds in glee.
He claims the victory.
He says, "I soon will take my throne,
and all will bow to me."
But then the battle starts to shift,
and soon the tide does turn.
Through power from an outside source,
the angels' hearts now burn.
A mighty fast has been proclaimed,
and Satan's army flees.
They can't withstand the mighty force
of saints upon their knees.
In other realms the spirits fight
the wars that pave our way.
None can defeat God's mighty troops
when Christians fast and pray.

KAPoe

Feeding Jesus

DEAR HEAVENLY FATHER

We thank You, God, for all You've done.
You gave us life. You sent Your Son.
You granted faith and righteousness.
And through Your mercy we are blessed.
We praise Your truthfulness and power,
The love and grace You give each hour.
We praise You for Your perfect ways.
Your perfect Light makes bright our days.
Forgive our sins, Lord, we beseech You.
Cleanse us, God, that we may reach You.
Our iniquities no more be shown
That we may come before Your throne.
Please bless our leaders You've appointed.
Grant them compassion for Your anointed.
Lord, heal and bless our families.
And build their faith, we ask You, please.
Through prayers and through our Bible search,
Let wisdom soon unite Your church.
And may our faith and victories won
Propel the masses to Your Son.
May Your Spirit grant us peace each day.
And teach us every godly way.

AMEN

KAPoe

Pride

Pride ✠ Contents

Feeding Jesus

GOD'S SHOVEL

There was a giant mound of dirt
where I began to dig.
Each scoop I took moved lots of earth.
My shovel was so big.
I worked real hard and took no breaks.
The hole grew fast and deep.
My work was so important there,
I took no time to sleep.
My arms were sore. I would not stop.
A cramp grew in my side.
But I was doing such big things
I overcame through pride.
The Lord must be so proud of me
and all this work I do.
I yelled out loud, "God look at me.
I'm glorifying You."
"I SEE THE WORK YOU'RE DOING THERE
THAT MAKES YOU FEEL SO BOLD.
BUT THE HOLE YOU DIG IS IN THE DIRT
ON THE SHOVEL THAT I HOLD."

Pride ✝ God's Shovel

KAPoe

201

Feeding Jesus

GOOD INTENTIONS

The love of God embraces all
His chosen family.
But if you choose Him not, you choose
to be His enemy.
You say you're good, and God is love.
"I don't steal, cheat, or lie.
If He's the God I've heard about,
my soul will never die."
The fact is you're already dead.
You're born under a curse.
If you don't give your heart to Christ,
you can expect the worst.
All righteousness in our own strength
are filthy rags that smell.
Our good intentions pave the road
that leads our soul to Hell.
God won't save the goodly souls
But those that He forgives.
So those who walk alone will die.
But those in Christ will live.

KAPoe

LETTING GO

There was a treasure in my grasp
I'd struggled hard to get.
God promised me a better prize.
I asked God, "What is it?"
He said, "Just put your faith in Me
and not what's in your hand.
Now cast your treasure at your feet.
Come see what I have planned."
Reluctantly, I let it go,
Though questioning my choice.
But for my Lord, I walked away
and followed His sweet voice.
I journeyed many days and nights
God's promises to find,
In earnest pushing from my thoughts
the treasure left behind.
I wondered, as I walked along,
what God's grand prize could be.
Then, like a sudden, brilliant light,
God's gift was shown to me.
It was a joy unspeakable
that welled up from inside.
The treasure I had left behind
was simply foolish pride.

KAPoe

Feeding Jesus

The Fix It Christian

Sometimes I make a giant mess
when I do things my way.
I jump in blindly with both feet
and don't take time to pray.
I try to be the fix it guy
when things tug at my heart.
But with no holy guidance,
my works can fall apart.
My heart takes over for my brain,
and wisdom is denied.
I open wide my mouth, in love,
and put my foot inside.
Then even if I speak the truth,
my words sometimes contend.
And so I make a bigger mess
than the one I tried to mend.
So please forgive my foolishness
when I think I'm so smart.
I pray that, like the Lord, you'll weigh
the intentions of my heart.

KAPoe

Another Chance

Dear God, forgive my foolish pride.
May I learn from my shame.
I blew another chance today
To glorify Your name.
Dear Lord, please help me be prepared.
Implant it in my heart
That I be poised with shield in hand
To face each evil dart.
Please keep Your Light before my eyes
In everything I do
That I might stay upon the path
I choose to walk for You.
Put so much love within my heart
That I can't even see
The paths to which the devil points
That lead away from Thee.
May all my steps be placed by You
And not by foolish pride
That all may see Your guiding hand,
And You'll be glorified.

KAPoe

Feeding Jesus

Feeding Jesus

Producing Fruit

KAPoe

Feeding Jesus

BLOOM

God chooses where each flower grows,
The color that it bears.
His love designs each leaf and stem,
The fragrance that it shares.
Its purpose is not one that's great.
It earns no grand reward.
But still each flower in each field
does glorify the Lord.
We have a purpose where we are
in every state and season.
Though finite minds can't comprehend,
The Father has a reason.
So use each day to serve the Lord
through gifts that you've been granted.
It doesn't matter where you are.
So bloom where you've been planted.

Producing Fruit ✚ Bloom

Feeding Jesus

CAST AGAIN

I cast my net upon the sea.
The whole of night I toil.
I draw it back and cast again.
My effort yields no spoil.
I stop and row my boat a ways.
Again my net I spread.
Reluctantly, I draw again
The empty net I dread.
I bow my head and pray awhile
For blessing from above.
I pray, Lord, fill my empty net
That more might know Your love.
The sea is Earth. My boat is Christ.
My net is God's sweet Word.
I cast again. I won't give up
Till everyone has heard.
My Savior stands upon the shore,
Beyond the ebbing tide.
Then at His Word I cast again
Upon the other side.

KAPoe

A Real Friend

I pray, dear God, please use me,
no matter what it takes,
to guide my neighbor to You.
A brother for to make.
Lord, give me the perfect words
I need to plant the seed.
Then may my brothers help me
give water that it needs.
But all our seeds are worthless
without Your Spirit though.
Because without His nurturing
those seeds will never grow.
Sometimes it takes disaster
to bring repentance true.
Sometimes we hit rock bottom
before we come to You.
Sometimes they may get angry,
and we may lose a friend.
But if they find salvation,
it's worth it in the end.
If I speak not and then they die,
what friend then would I be
to watch a loved one go to Hell
because I thought of me?

KAPoe

Feeding Jesus

Blessed Again

Jesus is our Lifeboat.
He rescued you and me.
So now we sit within our Boat
Upon the restless sea.
Drowning people all around us
Refuse to take our hand.
So now we must convince them
It's too far to swim to land.
This Boat's your only hope, we say.
Please let us pull you in.
For we don't want to see you drown
In deep waters of sin.
Blessed again, each time we pull
Another soul on board.
Continuously bearing fruit
As we work for the Lord.
There're millions in the water,
As far as you can see.
And every person that gets saved
Becomes your family.

212 KAPoe

Dig Deep

The house you build is your own life.
So build it strong to stay.
Dig way down deep within your heart
And love's foundation lay.
For love's the Rock you build upon.
This step can't be ignored.
Your house must stand the test of time.
The Rock is our sweet Lord.
With mercy, build your house with care.
With wisdom, make it strong.
Compassion makes a great front door,
With that you can't go wrong.
Then when the violent storms of life
Beat fiercely on your wall,
Your house is safe and warm inside.
God's grace won't let it fall.
Your family, within that house,
Will, in that Rock, believe.
And when they see those raging storms,
They will not want to leave.

Producing Fruit ✚ Dig Deep

ETERNAL FRIENDS

Won't you let me introduce you
to my most precious Friend?
He knows of your beginning
and how your life will end.
He knows what makes you happy
and all that makes you sad.
He wants to fill your heart with joy
More than you've ever had.
Before He had become my Friend
I was His enemy.
But that could not keep Him away
Because He still loved me.
He knows that you don't trust Him now.
He hopes that you will see
the evidence before your eyes
Of change He's made in me.
He knocks upon your heart's front door.
He pleads you let Him in.
He knows that when you open it,
your new life can begin.
You'll never find another friend
that loves you oh so true.
Before the day that you were born
my Friend had died for you.

KAPoe

FAIR WARNING

The wickedness of Nineveh
Came up before God's throne.
God's mercy overcame His wrath.
He sent one man alone.
An angry man who hated them
And hoped they wouldn't live
Brought them a warning from the Lord
He didn't want to give.
He was a Jew, their enemy.
This message he deployed.
"Yet forty days you have to live.
Then you will be destroyed."
Reaction was immediate.
And they proclaimed a fast.
They sat in ashes, and they prayed,
Repenting for their past.
Because of faith, and faith alone,
They heard the message shared.
They turned to God in fear and love,
And Nineveh was spared.
When God sends friends and family,
Whose love you know is true,
You'd better heed the words they say.
There's no excuse for you.

KAPoe

Feeding Jesus

God Watches

A tiny babe, alone and scared,
lay crying to be fed.
Blind and naked on the floor
with none to brace his head.
A multitude had come and gone.
Each one had passed him by.
So busy reaching for the prize,
They left him there to die.
This scene, that seems unthinkable,
God watches day by day.
So many perish in the dark
with none to guide the way.
Each sinner is that tiny babe
who's crying to be fed,
A precious diamond in the rough
for whom our Savior bled.
We cannot force the blind to see,
But God says "we must try."
Or else his blood will stain our hands
if we should pass him by.

KAPoe

Feeding Jesus

Reverence

Feeding Jesus

KAPoe

Feeding Jesus

Room For One

God stood before a prideful man.
He watched him day by day.
God led to him men of great faith,
But he sent them away.
God showed him many miracles.
The man refused to see.
He took the credit for them all.
He puffed his chest in glee.
He'd boast of his achievements
while living as he willed,
Refusing to acknowledge God
and all He has fulfilled.
He lived by what he saw and felt.
"I take what I receive.
Until I see God with my eyes,
I can't and won't believe."
God said, "LOOK FOR ME WITH YOUR HEART,
AND YOU'LL SEE ALL I'VE SHOWN.
BUT I CAN'T HELP YOU WHERE YOU ARE,
YOU'RE SITTING ON MY THRONE."

Reverence ✠ Room For One

KAPoe

Feeding Jesus

RENEWED

Jesus is the Resurrection,
the Path, the Life, the Way.
He holds the cross I'm carrying.
I die for Him each day.
Each time He gives me victory,
I die a little more.
Some day there'll be no memory
of the man I was before.
I die a little more to pride,
and lust, and hate, and greed
As Jesus fills my heart with love,
and faith, and grace I need.
As He increases in my life,
I decrease a little more.
Though once an enemy of God,
through Christ all peace restored.
I'll strive to glorify my Lord
in all I say and do.
Although I'm nothing on my own,
in Jesus I'm renewed.

KAPoe

Feeding Jesus

Salvation

Salvation ✚ Contents

Feeding Jesus

KAPoe

Feeding Jesus

My Day Of Life

My life begins and so the morn.
In sin conceived, in sin I'm born.
Confused and helpless, I rely
On what I'm given to get by.
Belief in lies the world does give
Becomes the rule for how I live.
I search and grope for joy to find.
Without a clue that I am blind.
At noon the sun does shine full power.
That I might see my darkest hour.
But in that dark, a Light I see.
A voice within is calling me.
The Light convicts me of my sin
That true repentance can begin.
Corrupt and loathsome, but contrite,
I give myself unto the Light.
He sanctifies and cleanses me,
Removing my iniquity.
The gift I'm given is my seed.
I plant to help a world in need.
I'll tell them of the love He's shown
Till comes the night He takes me home.

KAPoe

Feeding Jesus

PAINLESS

God sent a message on the wind
unto my heart to say,
He's thinking of you in your pain.
He's reaching out this day.
He's sent you many messengers.
He watches from above.
He hopes that you will come to Him
That you may know His love.
He knows of your infirmities,
Your heartache, and your strife.
He is your only hope for joy
in this depressing life.
His children bow and pray to Him.
"Dear God, show us the way
to lead this man unto Your throne
To be Your son today."
Your sorrow makes the Savior weep.
You're suffering in vain.
He knocks upon your heart's front door.
He wants to ease your pain.
No matter where you've won or failed,
No matter what you've done,
The God of mercy waits for you
to love you as a son.

KAPoe

A Better Plan

Where is it that you think you'll go,
Oh follower of men?
Where is it that you think you'll be
When your short life here ends?
People falling in the dark
Can't lend a helping hand.
So if you've put your faith in them,
You need a better plan.
No great worldly reputation
Can keep your body well.
And abundant wealth can't save you
From the darkest depths of Hell.
Your soul belongs to Satan
Or else to God above.
It's going to die by fire
Or live forever in God's love.
So give your heart to Jesus Christ
Or go play with your friends.
But don't say nobody warned you
When your play time on Earth ends.

Salvation ✝ A Better Plan

Feeding Jesus

A Different Road

I used to walk a different road.
My path was smooth and wide.
The easy way was always best.
So downhill did I stride.
And then a fork was in the road.
There stood a Man in white.
He said, "THAT ROAD WILL LEAD TO DEATH.
YOU NEED TO MAKE A RIGHT."
He offered me a narrow path
Of rocks and hills and work.
Why would I trade all this for that?
He must think I'm a jerk.
So on I go the way I was,
But very soon I find,
The rocky path, the Man in white,
Are constant on my mind.
Again I came unto a fork.
This time it was at night.
My mind could not believe my eyes.
The path was in the Light.
The Man in white said, "FOLLOW ME
BECAUSE FOR YOU I'M SENT.
BELIEVE THAT I CAN GIVE YOU LIFE
IF YOU WILL JUST REPENT."

KAPoe

Feeding Jesus

So now I walk among the rocks
And hills that make me strong.
And there's no doubt within my mind,
I'm right where I belong

Salvation ✠ A Different Road

A Real Man

The world says you're a weakling
If you surrender or submit.
You'll lose control and power,
And this you can't permit.
But ponder for a moment
This next thing that I say.
The devil only lets you think
You do things your own way.
But in truth he holds the reins.
He leads you from reward.
You need to take them from his hand
And give them to the Lord.
It's strength to let the demons say
You must not be a man.
True courage lets God lead you blind
Through the glory of His plan.
Any fool can be led by rage
And give in to his pride.
But a real man, with true control,
Can let God be his guide.

KAPoe

BUTTERFLIES

Born a caterpillar,
Into this life we're hurled.
Oblivious to surroundings,
Devouring our world,
Blindly eating every leaf
That comes into our sight.
Judging goodness by our taste,
Not knowing wrong from right,
But God's Word wrapped tight around us.
Enclosed in His cocoon,
Separated from those worldly views,
Our souls begin to bloom.
Then we emerge in joy and peace
That Satan's will denies.
No longer all consuming worms
But Heaven's butterflies.

KAPoe

Feeding Jesus

CAN'T BE DONE

If you're waiting for some special day,
You'll feel compelled to live God's way.
Then in the strength that's yours alone,
You'll earn the right to see God's throne.
I tell you now it can't be done.
The Way to God is through His Son.
Without the Lord, try as you might,
You're doomed to wage a fruitless fight.
God doesn't save the righteous man.
He makes you righteous through His plan.
Don't wait until you're good enough.
You'll never get that far.
He knows you need His guiding hand.
He'll take you as you are.
Just put your faith in Him alone
And turn from things you do.
If you will put Him on your throne,
Then He will strengthen you.

KAPoe

CHOOSE LIFE

God does not lead to confusion.
He's not a God of strife.
He's made it clear there's but one way
To have eternal life.
Confusion is the devil's way
To keep us in our sin.
False doctrines twist and turn our path
Like waves pushed by the wind.
So Satan offers many roads
To keep us in a daze
That we might be forever lost
Within his evil maze.
So many will reach out to God.
In vain will many pray.
But only Jesus holds the key,
So few will find the way.
All good deeds done in our own strength,
Of which the sinner brags,
Can never wipe away the bad.
They're simply filthy rags.
The Gospel is the gospel truth.
All others will deceive.
No other way than Christ the Lord,
In Him we must believe.

KAPoe

Salvation ✠ Choose Life

Feeding Jesus

His followers will win the race,
But other souls will lose.
A righteous God won't bless them all.
Be careful what you choose.

Salvation ✚ Choose Life

KAPoe

Don't Wait

God's not here to prove Himself
to those who won't believe.
They'd not accept Him anyway.
They'd say they've been deceived.
Jesus healed, and raised the dead
right under human eyes.
Still their hearts would not have faith,
And still their hearts denied.
If you're waiting for a miracle,
then you are truly lost.
Jesus was God's miracle.
We nailed Him to a cross.
God's already proved Himself.
His love took the first step.
Now your only hope is faith.
His love you must accept.
All our hopes and dreams in life,
God's love for us exceeds.
Just the fact we live and breathe
is all the proof we need.

KAPoe

Feeding Jesus

HIS LIGHT MINE

I was lost and all seemed hopeless.
Only clocks and dogs
Made noise to split the night.
Tempers flared and senses reeling.
Soft words spoken had no meaning.
Life was just a long and boring fight.
Then our sweet Lord in Heaven above
Came to my heart and spread His love.
Then all at once I seemed to have new sight.
The little things that used to slay me
Don't upset and don't dismay me.
I am quite content within His Light.

KAPoe

Shame

Feeding Jesus

KAPoe

ANCHORS AWAY

Don't ever waste a moment.
Hold each one dear and fast.
Don't ruin now or future
because of something past.
God said He'd take my sins away,
My guilt and all my shame.
But if I will not let it go,
true joy my heart won't gain.
Not only, though, the things I've done
but what's been done to me.
I must release it from my grip
so God can set me free.
These things are like an anchor
That binds me to the shore.
God offers me an ocean.
He wants me to explore.
He waits here to remove my chains,
To open doors and bands.
But sadly they are locked in place.
The keys are in my hands.

KAPoe

Feeding Jesus

The Rooster Crowed

I didn't take my trial to Christ.
I relied on what I know.
And somewhere deep inside my heart
I heard a rooster crow.
I try to help a friend alone.
My stress and anger grow.
Again I hear that awful sound.
Again the rooster crowed.
I tried to hide something I'd done
and not confess my sin.
My heart was crushed this time I heard
the rooster crow again.
And so I wallowed in my shame,
A pain so sure to last.
And so I left with head held low,
Returning to my past.
There stood a Man upon the shore.
He beckoned I come near.
I felt a strength rise up in me
That overcame my fear.
Three times He asked me of my love.
My heart within me cried.
He took away the shame I felt
That Him I'd thrice denied.

KAPoe

UNFORGIVEN

I've forgiven all that's done to me.
The hatred's gone. I've set it free.
I'm never known to hold a grudge.
But in this one case, my heart won't budge.
May God forgive me if I sin.
My stubborn conscience won't give in.
Though God forgives him from above,
This man has hurt someone I love.
I hope that in the time I live,
Someday this man my heart forgives.
When I forgive a man, it sets me free.
But it's harder when...that man is me.

Shame ✚ Unforgiven

KAPoe

239

Feeding Jesus

Feeding Jesus

Sowing And Reaping

Feeding Jesus

KAPoe

BANK OF HEAVEN

Seems every time I put me first
I fall right on my face.
Whenever I demand the best,
I'm not living in faith.
God says, "To get good things from Him,
We'll have to sow to reap."
That means the more we give away
the more we get to keep.
We build treasures in Heaven
by meeting others' needs.
But all our stuff remains behind
that we have kept in greed.
The seeds we plant while we are here
will grow in Kingdom fields.
The more we plant upon the Earth
the more the Kingdom yields.
So if you hide your treasures,
they're yours until you're dead.
But you can't take it with you,
So send it on ahead.

GARDENING

I see a garden, bright and green.
The hedges trimmed, the paths are clean.
The roses pruned, well watered too.
The beds are raked, so much to do.
You'd have to search to find a weed.
This garden gets the love it needs.
The gardener, so diligent,
Gets great reward for time he's spent.
But he must labor every day
Or soon such beauty fades away.
Your garden won't grow by itself.
It's up to you and no one else.
So give it water, spread your seeds.
And don't forget to pull your weeds.
Great blessings come in what you've grown.
But gardens won't grow on their own.
Your Christian walk is much the same,
But the flower there is Jesus' name.

KAPoe

SEARCHING

I lived so many years alone
within this crowded place.
For it was me against the world,
My heart devoid of grace.
No true-blue friends I'd ever known
Nor had I known true love.
I searched in blindness with my hands,
but never looked above.
I used the people in my life
to gain the joy I sought.
But all my efforts were in vain,
And joy my heart knew not.
In desperation to be loved
I reached out to the Lord.
"Please fill this dark and empty heart
or let death be my reward."
God said, "DON'T SEARCH FOR JOY OR LOVE,
BUT SPREAD IT AS YOU GO.
LOVE IS A SEED YOU NEED TO PLANT,
THEN YOU'LL REAP WHAT YOU SOW."
My heart has peace to finally know,
when comes my final breath,
that those on Earth who know me best
might truly mourn my death.

KAPoe

Feeding Jesus

Feeding Jesus

Spiritual Gifts

Feeding Jesus

KAPoe

Bright Lights

The Spirit gives to each of us
a gift from God above,
a gift to lift and guide and help,
That all might know God's love.
And so, in faith, we share each gift,
a light upon the hill.
In love and earnestness we strive
to do the Father's will.
Don't hide your talents in the ground,
Preserving it for naught.
For when the Spirit sees the waste,
He'll take that which you've got.
To faithful servants He will give
the gift you've buried deep.
Because they know the more they give
the more they get to keep.
And so they shine that light so bright
the world can't help but see.
And their gifts are irrevocable,
to share eternally.

KAPoe

Feeding Jesus

Feeding Jesus

Thanksgiving

Feeding Jesus

KAPoe

Feeding Jesus

Grace For Grace

Our Savior took and broke the bread
and lifted it to God.
And though a deity Himself,
He didn't think it odd.
For everything on Earth is God's,
Although you feel you've earned it.
And all true wisdom comes from Him,
Regardless where we've learned it.
The Father loves a thankful heart.
Our praise to Him we lift,
a sweet aroma to the Lord.
We thank Him for each gift.
In earnestness of heart we pray
His grace and blessings flow
to every hungry soul in need
That His great love may show.
So take your gift of gratitude
and lay it at His throne
For what we eat that gives us life
and all the love He's shown.

Thanksgiving ✚ Grace For Grace

KAPoe

Feeding Jesus

MANY THANKS

I hope God never tires of thanks
I've given Him before.
For some things once is not enough.
And so I thank Him more.
I thank Him for church family
and the love, through them, He's shown.
A pure, sweet love I never knew
till I came to His throne.
For this I can't thank Him enough.
I strive to make it grand.
And so I've thanked Him many times.
I hope He understands.
It's not so much the things they give
or each delicious meal.
It's more the fact they really care
and all the love I feel.
And so, dear Lord, please brace Yourself
'Cause here it comes again.
I thank You, God, with all my heart
for every one of them.

KAPoe

PERSPECTIVE

A rich man and a poor man
whose lifelong paths had crossed.
The poor man there because of gain,
The rich man through his loss.
They shared a room, not great nor grand,
All luxury denied.
Sufficient shelter from the snow.
Dry, safe, and warm inside.
They had only the food they'd need.
No extra could they spare.
The roof was sound, the water clean,
the stove in good repair.
Each day the rich man, on his cot,
Would cry out to the Lord.
"Why, God, have You forsaken me
and taken my reward?"
Each day, the poor man, on his knees,
with arms stretched high and wide,
He praised the Lord for blessing him.
Through tears of joy he cried.

KAPoe

Feeding Jesus

Feeding Jesus

Truth

Truth ✚ Contents

Feeding Jesus

BALANCED

If we had grace but not the truth,
We'd be licensed to kill.
If we had truth but not God's grace,
We could not do His will.
We need the truth to show us how
to glorify the Lord,
To guide us in the race we run
That leads to God's reward.
Without God's grace, darkness prevails.
No Light shines where we look.
Without forgiveness of our sins
the Bible's just a book.
We need the balance of the two
to guide and light the way.
Without them both there'll be no works
to test on judgment day.
So read your Bible every day
and thank God for His grace.
By grace all doers of the Word
Will someday see God's face.

Truth + Balanced

KAPoe

Feeding Jesus

Unlock The Mystery

It's grace that brings eternal life.
But works that build our crown.
In being doers of the Word
Our Heaven's treasure's found.
Except a man be born again
God's kingdom he won't see.
No other way for us to join
the Father's family.
Then when we love each other dear
as children of the Lord,
in unity we work as one
to earn our grand reward.
The Bible holds salvation's plan.
The Word's our only key.
No other book, doctrine, or god
Unlocks the mystery.
If Jesus Christ is in your heart,
Then you will have the proof.
For then the Spirit of the Lord
Will guide you in all truth.
The greatest members of the church
Will serve most humbly.
And if you know and do these things,
Then happy will you be.

KAPoe

BUILD ON ROCK

There are things that will go with you
And things that stay behind.
Let peace and wisdom, faith and love,
Be foremost in your mind.
Build upon these things each day
for these you get to keep.
All the rest remains behind
When comes the final sleep.
Peace comes from believing
The things that God's assured.
And wisdom comes from studying
The Father's precious Word.
Your faith will build upon your faith
Each time the Lord comes through.
And love you'll build by spreading love
the Savior gives to you.
So gather friends and neighbors
And bring them to the Lord.
Then when we get to Heaven,
Your heart God will reward.

Feeding Jesus

Feeding Jesus

Virtue

Feeding Jesus

THE VIRTUOUS WOMAN

The virtuous woman this man sees
Is far more precious than rubies.
His praise of her stems from this must,
His contented heart can safely trust.
She does him kind, no evil there,
Through all the days they're blessed to share.
Like merchant ships from many lands,
She brings food and toils with her sweet hands.
Before the sun her love prepares
Meals for her household that she shares.
So needy men can drink and sup,
She'll place her coins in their tin cups.
She fears not snow for her household.
Her love does clothe them from the cold.
Adorned with silk and lace and stuff,
As though her beauty weren't enough.
With dignity and wisdom on her tongue,
She teaches kindness to her young.
Her children clean, well-fed, and dressed
by the loving mother with whom they're blessed.
Thank God the woman I adore
Loves, believes, and fears the Lord.
Though excellent women line the walls,
You, my love, surpass them all.

KAPoe

THE DASH

We're born and live and then we pass.
We're then placed in the ground.
Above us, loved ones put a stone.
On it, our story's found.
It says our name and then beloved
Dad, Mother, daughter, son.
Between the dates we're born and died,
a dash for all we've done.
It's not our place to choose our birth
or how or when we'll die.
But we will choose who we will serve
and how we spend our lives.
We give our lives to Christ in love
and store up Heaven's treasures.
Or seek great riches on the Earth
to spend on worldly pleasures.
No matter how long that we live,
It's over in a flash.
Our legacy is all that's left.
It's all there in the dash.

KAPoe

Feeding Jesus

Worry

Feeding Jesus

KAPoe

His Rest

When the Lord said, "COME, ENTER MY REST,"
He didn't mean lay down.
But in tranquility of mind
the Father's rest is found.
We can't enjoy His blessings
at the table God prepares.
Each tender morsel has no taste
until we cast our cares.
Our worry is a type of faith
that darkness will prevail.
But true faith shines a light so bright
we see God's Word won't fail.
For the Savior's yoke is easy.
In it we share His might.
He toils with us, side by side.
And so the burden's light.
Our worry cannot steer the ship.
The Captain's in control.
In strife, we strike out at the air.
In faith, God rests our soul.

Worry ✠ His Rest

KAPoe

Feeding Jesus

KAPoe

About The Author

Born in Detroit, Michigan, in 1959 he has lived in California all of his life. For the most part abandoned at age five to be raised by strangers in foster homes and group placements, he was raised without remarkable Christian guidance. Because he didn't trust adults, he received most of his guidance and moral principles from peers who were as lost as he was. He lived a life he is far from proud of until he accepted Jesus Christ as his Lord and Savior while kneeling on a cold concrete floor in a county jail. For the past ten years, he has devoted his life to learning and serving the Lord's will with all his heart. With no knowledge, training, or interest in the art of poetry, God has used him to glorify Himself through the least of men. His poetry has led many men throughout the California prison system to begin, renew, or enrich a meaningful relationship with the Lord. Please join him in praying that those men will truly be transformed by the renewing of their minds.

"To order more copies of this book, please send an email request to *FeedingJesusBook@yahoo.com* with the desired shipping address and you will receive an email invoice."

59056192R00150

Made in the USA
Charleston, SC
25 July 2016